Christian Babe Alert

Dan Vasi

Amherst, OH

Christian Babe Alert

This book is a work of non-fiction. All rights reserved. No part of this publication may be copied, reproduced, stored, archived or transmitted in any form or by any means without prior written permission from the publisher, except in the case of brief quotations used for articles and reviews.

Copyright © 2013 by Dan Vasi
Cover Art © 2013 by Neal Seamus
Edited by Jennifer Midkiff

This work was compiled by the author through personal experience, interviews, and research. Although the author and publisher have researched the information contained in this book, we assume no responsibility for errors, inaccuracies, omissions, or any inconsistency herein.

Loconeal Publishing can bring authors to your live event.
Loconeal books may be ordered through booksellers or by contacting:
www.loconeal.com
216-772-8380

First Loconeal Publishing edition: March, 2013

ISBN 978-0-9885289-5-6 (Trade Paperback)

Acknowledgement

Thanks to my Father, Jesus Christ, for sticking with this hardheaded boy. Thank you to my sexy, hot babe, Erin Michelle, for loving me the way God intended. Thanks to my long-time friend, Gary, for your countless hours of help.

Table of Contents

BABE ALERT! 1
   GROUNDWORK 2
   TEST DRIVING THE LADIES 5
   WILL I EVEN LIKE HER 12

INTERVIEW ONE 15
   DISCUSSING THE BASICS WITH FOUR HISPANIC HOTTIES

INTERVIEW DOS (2) 47
   TWO STAGGERING BEAUTIES TELL ME ALL ABOUT ROMANCE

INTERVIEW TROIS (3) 84
   SNOT-NOSED SISTER INTO INSIGHTFUL SIBLING

INTERVIEW VIER (4) 109
   THE FINAL INTERVIEW
   DISCOVERING DATING IN THE MIDST OF A WINTER
      WONDERLAND

BABES BEWARE 147

POST STORY 152

INTERVIEW QUESTIONS FOR DISCUSSION 155
   FIRST INTERVIEW 156
   SECOND INTERVIEW 157
   THIRD INTERVIEW 158
   FOURTH INTERVIEW 159

BABE ALERT!

"You're so cute and I just wanted to know if you would go out with me?" Chances are, if you've picked up this book you wouldn't mind a hot, young woman asking you that very question. Ever since I turned 17 and started following Jesus, I've desperately searched for that special someone. Now, at 26, I finally . . . . decided to write this book. (You were probably expecting me to say how I finally found that perfect girl and how I am now happily married.)

Nope, I'm still as single as ever.

That's why I determined to write a book that consisted of me asking stunning, Christian women all of the questions that us guys long to know the answers to. I got the idea to interview women one day as I thought about a new Bible on the market.

I remember the first day that the Bible came out. It was titled "Revolve," and it was actually the New Testament wrapped up in a magazine-like cover. If you've ever seen Revolve (as you probably have considering it became the best-selling Bible that year in less than three months after it was released), then you know it is made for young women.

Ok, so the Bible looked like a fat magazine and it had a pinkish cover with a girl on the front, yet I was still drawn in.

When I first caught sight of it, I was working through my shift as a salesman at Family Christian Stores. Someone had just set up our eye-catching display of the pretty, little publication. I looked around to see if anyone was watching, then I made a dash for the shelf. I clearly remember glancing through the slick pages and stopping every time I saw one of the numerous articles where a girl would tell what she thought about guys. It was so cool because, for the first time, I was getting information straight from the horse's mouth, so to speak. Actually it was a much prettier mouth.

At that time, I had read between six and nine gazillion books about ladies written by leading male authors, and they had all helped me tremendously. *But what if I wrote a book where I actually interviewed Christian babes*, I thought. Now that would be awesome! And hey, I might even find mine along the way.

In a nutshell, that's how this book came to be. As you can see, it didn't stem from completely selfless ambitions, but it will unquestionably encourage and motivate most of you single guys out there. Before I bust into the interviews, let me lay a little groundwork about the predicament us lonesome guys often find ourselves in.

Groundwork

Christian guys everywhere are striving to be the hero of a woman's heart. They want to find the girl that is beautiful and makes them feel strong. Unfortunately, the problem is: the search is not all that easy. There are so many lovely ladies, but there's always something wrong. "She's too pretty for me," you might say. You're attracted to her, but not sure if she knows

Jesus (Yeah, been there). The girl has a great attitude, but you just don't feel fascinated with her looks. It's all so confusing, right?

Yes, love is perplexing and when all those doubts arise, us men tend to run to the extremes. For instance, there are guys like me on the one extreme who are so hesitant to make a mistake, you're more likely to find them playing video games than talking to the opposite sex (Not that gaming is bad. I love it more than my own life, after all. I mean, Zelda and Call of Duty? C'mon). We (read: wimps) don't necessarily hide from women, we just feel as though God is going to beam one down right in front of us when He's good and ready. You know, one day while we're at a Redbox (movie vending machine) hunting for the last copy of the newest super-hero movie, we'll just happen to glance up. Our jaw hinge will swing open as we see this glowing light from Heaven cascading over this fine-looking girl as the angels sing in harmony.

POP! Chances are it ain't going to happen.

Yes, us wimps all know that such a thing is unrealistic, but we tend to tell ourselves that God will somehow let us know when the right girl comes along. The cool thing is, He will. The problem? Well, it's not like we think. We hope that as long as we visit the physical world once in a while (for example, to go to the gas station, or the grocery store, or even the mall to buy video games), God will give us that old nudge to the soul and say, "THAT'S THE ONE, TIGER." It may happen like that, and for your sake, I hope it does. For the majority of us, however, God expects a little more from us. The fact of the matter is that God will direct us, but we've got to be moving for that to happen.

To represent this idea, consider the following, colorful analogy. Let's say that one day while you are walking down the sidewalk, feeling kinda lonely, a crazy old man suddenly pulls up next to you. As his '82 station wagon's engine putters, he asks you how he could get to somewhere where he could buy a shirt. *That's weird*, you think, as you spit out the directions to your local Walmart. Then, suddenly the old man turns his car off. To your surprise he yells, "OK, I don't see it!" "You've got to drive down the street and make a right at the light," you repeat. Then he screams, "I need to buy a shirt; show me the shirt!" At that point you turn and run for your life (Don't be embarrassed; we all get scared sometimes.)

The point is that when we want a shirt (or in our case, a skirt) God will give us directions to where they are. Does God have a skirt that will fit you perfectly? (Whoa, this is getting a little weird.) Yes, God knows what woman will fit you best and He will be happy to introduce you to her. The trick is that you have to be moving to where she is and not sitting still if you intend to find her.

To solidify this point, check out how Isaac got his babe in Genesis 24. Abraham, Isaac's pops knew it was about time for his son to get a wife. Abraham sent his oldest and most trusted servant to his homeland to find a wife for Isaac. Abraham had direction from God to send his servant to a certain place to find his son's wife-to-be. Although Abraham didn't know what girl his servant would find or how he would locate her, he just knew that it was time to get moving. He told his servant that God "will send his angel ahead of you, and he will see to it that you find a young woman there to be my son's wife," (Gen. 24:7). Abraham was the man declared righteous by God because of his faith (in Genesis 15:6) so naturally it would be an excellent idea to follow his initiative.

If you are like me and have become paralyzed in your search for a woman, scared of failure or missing God's will, then this book is for you, my friend. Will you have to make a scary journey into the unknown? Probably. Don't fear, God has already sent his angel ahead of you to take care of the details.

I, along with many other guys, tend to reside in the Land of Fuzzy Creatures. Our homeland is lush and bright but the pink bunnies and the blue bears rarely ever meet. But not everyone lives in this land. Some men inhabit the Ville of Late Night Cartoons. They are the other extremists. In their world everything is sexy and sleek and smells like cologne. The Johnny Bravos are always on the hot pursuit of any hottie that moves.

Let's talk about these other extremists, the fellas on the opposite end of the spectrum from myself. You know, the little Puff Diddys that don't exhibit a bit of apprehension when it comes to asking a girl out. There are plenty of guys out there like that that have come to the conclusion that the only way to find the right girl is to date them all. It kind of makes sense. All guys that have ever had the luxury of purchasing a new car know that you don't just look around the car lot and say, "That red one looks charming, I'll take it!" When you find a car that intrigues you, you test drive it. That is the only logical way to find the car that works for you. Why not test drive the ladies, so to speak? Again, that is hinting at what God wants us to do, but it's not in the way you might be picturing.

Test Driving the Ladies

To illustrate my point, I want to take a quick flashback to my not-so-distant past. When I was about 18, my dad (who is a car miracle worker) got me this wrecked '95 Mustang that he said he would fix up for me. About a year later the car was still sitting in my dad's garage and let's just say my poor baby was hurting. My dad had told me many times he would have it done in the next week only to disappoint me.

At about age 20, my dad told me that if he didn't get it done that particular week, he would help me buy a new car. Of course, I didn't have money for a new car, but hey, I couldn't pass up a deal like that. As the next week passed by and my little, white Mustang still sat there almost dead, my dad actually decided to pay up on our little wager. He took me to the dealership. While we were there, I got to test drive a brand new Mustang Cobra. Okay, so my dad drove and I sat in the passenger seat. I could barely see over the beastly hood as the engine rumbled the ground. The car was a beautiful red and was quickly winning my heart.

After the smooth, exhilarating ride the salesman went to get us a loan and I had a seat in a white plastic chair in the waiting room. As I sat there anxiously, God asked me, "Why are you trying to get this car? I already gave you a car." My heart sank, but I knew what I had to do.

To this day, my custom-painted Mustang (yes my dad finished it) has been an awesome blessing to me. From my story, maybe you can see that test-driving doesn't always show us what is best for us; it just shows what we want the most. To all of you guys flirting with every girl that will pay attention to you, pull the reins in and check out how to find the right one. For your own good, soak up the wisdom behind this story and you might not want to compare dating a woman to test driving a car again!

As I stated earlier, God wants us to get moving in the right direction. To do that, we've got to go where the godly women are. Ok, so the old man got to Walmart, now what? We need further assistance, just like he would. The old dude, if he were smart, would ask the cashier where the shirts were located in order to save time and effort. In the world of shopping, losing a few minutes is not a big deal (just ask my mom). In our spiritual dating adventure, however, not knowing what we are looking for or where to find it can be costly and painful. In essence, I'm telling you to get moving and to slow down.

The thing that I have noticed about the way God works is that He is very balanced. As humans, we often maintain an all or nothing attitude. God, on the other hand, knows exactly what we need to do. As funny as it is true, it is rarely zilch and never all things. God has laid out His plan for us to encounter our babe in such a way that we have to be in motion, but also following his timely directions.

We guys know this feeling all too well. Let's take getting to your friend's new house that's out in the middle of WhotheHeckKnowsWhereville, for example. You would probably get directions from him over the phone while jotting down various locales. By the time the conversation ended, you would have a rough idea of how to get there. I say rough because guys tend to keep taking the directions even though they didn't fully understand some of them. Better that than actually letting another guy know you don't know where something is. Afterwards, you would head out on the road. Good. You've started the journey (even though the directions were a little fuzzy.) Then, an hour later, you call your friend back to see if you should've gotten off at that last exit.

He'll say, "Yeah, now turn right at the tracks and call me if you get lost."

It's not that God can't give perfect directions such as: "LISTEN SON! WALK INTO THE SPEEDWAY AT 10:32 AM AND REACH FOR A NEWSPAPER." Then, as soon as you do, your sweater gets tangled in this babe-licious girl's braces. God could certainly lead you down a path of never-ending, good coincidences that granted you everything you ever desired if He so chose to. The fact is that God often chooses to give us partial directions for whatever reason (Maybe so we'll actually talk to Him more often.)

Let's take a look back at Abraham's servant to see how these partial directions work. When the servant finally got to the town where Abraham told him to go, he made his camels kneel down beside a well. It was evening and the servant was most likely dusty and tired. He looked around and saw some women coming out to get some water from the well. Here was his chance, right? I mean the servant overcame being a wimp by making the journey to where the women were. That's more than I would have done, and I'm sure it wasn't easy for him, either! Check out what he said to Abraham before he left: "But suppose I can't find a young woman who will travel so far from home? May I then take Isaac there to live among your relatives?"

Sound familiar? It seems pretty similar to many of my own compromising thoughts. "But suppose I can't find a girl that's interested in me? Can I just wait until I'm really sure she likes me by watching her from afar?" Yeah, that's something like what I would say. If it were up to me, I would've probably let those doubts talk me into not going at all. I'm positive there are plenty of guys just like me that use any such excuse to stop their journey before it even begins. They use the "I-can't-go-to-work-today-there-might-be-a-lion-in-the-road" justification from Proverbs 26:13. You see, when we are too cautious in awaiting the perfect time, we never get anything done. We can always find something that's wrong with any particular moment.

Abraham's servant did the right thing by not letting his doubts hinder him. We all have doubts about what God wants us to accomplish from time to time, but we just need to tell them where to go. Yes, I'm talking about Hell (after all, that's where their daddy, the father of lies, is going to be pretty soon). I'm not saying that when a doubt arises you should scream at the top of your lungs, "Be vanquished to hell, foul spirit!" What I am saying is that when you have a doubt about what you know God has led you to do, pretend it's like a nasty spider crawling on your arm, and swat it away!

So anyway, the servant left his comfort zone to go to God's comfort zone. In other words, he got moving. Now there were all of these pretty ladies just walking his way (even if they were ugly, he couldn't tell because it was nighttime.) If it was up to our second breed of guys, who love 'em all, it would have been good pickin's. This is where the servant shows us the key to the whole balance issue. Abraham's servant had gotten as far as he could go with the partial directions he had received and now needed further guidance.

If you are the kind of guy that sees a pretty girl smile at you and thinks that's God's guidance then you need to pay close attention here. There were plenty of eligible women at the well that night just like there would be a ton of roads to choose from once you ran out of directions going over to your friend's house. Just as you would have the sense (hopefully) to call your friend, the servant asks God to further clarify. Even though he had traveled all that way to find a woman and now the women were flocking to him like seagulls to French fries, he didn't maintain control of the love coupé. Instead, he slowed it down and let God take command. In this respect Abraham's servant displayed the same type of balance both of our groups of extremists need to strive for when searching for their babes.

Trust me when I say that I realize how hard it is to stop and ask for guidance when you think you have everything under control. Sometimes we take the initial drive from God, then run with it even when we burn out of gas. God is telling us to refuel, but we don't want to get out of the driver's seat. Sometimes we love the way things are going so much that it can be very hard to stop. It's almost as hard as a seven year-old skidding his feet down a curly slide in order to halt in the middle. (Don't tell me I'm the only one to have ever done that.)

Okay, so these girls were pouring out towards this servant who was looking for a girl, right? Then, all of a sudden, the servant prayed, "O Lord, God of my master. Give me success and show kindness to my master, Abraham. Help me to accomplish the purpose of my journey. See, here I am, standing beside this spring, and the young women of the village are coming out to draw water. This is my request. I will ask one of them for a drink. If she says 'Yes, certainly, and I will water your camels too!'—let her be the one you have appointed as Isaac's wife."

That prayer was a big deal! It showed that the servant knew when to slow down and ask for direction. After all, he had made it so far and God's answer was beginning to become clearer, like washing one side of a window. The servant could have been happy and just searched through the girls for the best possible wife. This servant was wise, though. He knew that he had begun to wash the one side of the window when he initially got moving, but he knew there was a more difficult part coming up. How many of you guys know that washing the inside of a window is cake compared to going outside and windexing the splattered bug guts on the other side? (Who am I kidding? Like we clean windows.) The hard part comes when you get to your destination (whether it is going to church, out with groups of Christian pals, etc.) and recognize that you now have to trust in God for the next move. Could you take control of the situation by yourself, now that you know all of these young ladies? Sure, but just don't expect God's great outcome.

Now we understand that we need to take the initial 'leap of faith' to God's women and then follow God's lead into the good stuff, but who are we supposed to imitate? Abraham? His servant? Or maybe Isaac? Well in actuality, all three should be accounted for.

Back in such ancient times when Abraham lived, the parents usually chose a son's wife. Since I'm sure none of you guys want that to happen now, we have to take on the role of the servant. We have to listen to God like the servant listened to Abraham. We have to go where God tells us to go. We also have to carry out the role of Isaac in accepting who God gives us. Therefore, the role that Abraham had in telling his servant when and where to go represents what God will do in our very own lives. We must take initiative when God tells us to, ask for instruction when we are unsure, and embrace what God gives us.

Will I Even Like Her?

Don't worry about God giving you something you don't want. Just check out how the Bible explains Isaac's girl, Rebekah. The Bible says as the servant was still praying, "a young woman named Rebekah arrived with a water jug on her shoulder . . . . Now Rebekah was *very beautiful,* and she was a virgin;" That should reassure you and fill you with hope. God placed that burning desire for a beautiful woman inside your heart with the intent to fulfill it.

The verse also mentioned Rebekah being a virgin. This was to expose the fact that she was pure, not perfect. Rebekah had her faults, as every person does, but her heart was right with God. If you are earnestly seeking to please God, then He will supply you with a woman that is likewise pure of heart.

Don't think for a second that you have to find a girl with a flawless track record, i.e. a physical virgin. I mean that's really awesome if you do, but it's far more important to be pure in heart now than having been pure in deeds for an eternity past. After all, our heart is what gets us into Heaven, not our deeds.

A girl that lives with a pure heart now, will definitely produce good works. Even if that same girl has done some sinful stuff with guys in the past. On the other hand, a girl that has stayed a virgin for the wrong reasons (maybe to boast about her chastity) doesn't necessarily have a right heart with God.

Unfortunately, this book isn't really written to help you with God's direction to your unique girl. (Sorry about that.) Don't worry though, this book will help you get prepared to enter the world of women so that God can point out your very own Christian babe. We are all going to have to communicate with women before we discover the one God has for us. Being in contact with women is tough, especially when you are trying to impress them in a godly manner. Women are mysterious, often leaving us fumbling for our words just by merely being in their presence. They are pinnacles of beauty and yet there is much we need to learn about them.

I know that this has been one heck of an introduction, but there is just a little more before we break into the locked chests of women's thoughts. Understand that although I think I know a lot about women, I really don't. In order to get to my Walmart (where the ladies are) I grasped the fact that I must know more about these seductive creatures.

I suppose it's kind of like my dog. I think I know exactly what she's thinking. The fact is, if she could talk she would probably be like, "Dang dude, if you don't stop talking to me in that squirrelly, little voice I'm going to put a Chihuahua-bite-down on your big head." The groovy thing is, girls can talk (a lot, I found out). And rather like how I construed my dog, they want to tell us some pretty unexpected advice.

That is the reason I decided to brave the World of Women and interview quite a few enchanting, strong Christian women (Yes, interviewing hot, Christian women was strenuous, but I unselfishly did it for the good of mankind.) I asked these young ladies every question I could conjure up so that their answers might better prepare us searching men and give us the confidence we need to go where God is calling us. You will not believe the jewels of wisdom that I have uncovered. I guess that's why Solomon wrote the proverb, "The man who finds a wife finds a treasure and receives favor from the Lord."

Without further ado, I want to present you with all of my

findings, taken from many great hours in the presence of some women that will make wonderful future wives for a bunch of special guys. These young women have taught me a lot that I wanted to pass on to you. I also included a good dose of my own wisdom (much of which was gained by reading a truckload of Proverbs). In reading these interviews, I hope and pray that God will open your hearts to everything you need to know to begin your first and final quest. It is now easy to see why Solomon, the wisest man who ever lived, portrayed wisdom as a "she."

INTERVIEW ONE

DISCUSSING THE BASICS WITH FOUR HISPANIC HOTTIES

Babe Talk

Gum versus Mints.
Out of twenty babes surveyed:
45% said they prefer when a guy chews gum,
50% said they like it when a guy sucks on mints,
and 5% said it doesn't matter.
"To me—when a guy chews gum—it's a turn on."
—Vanessa

Discussing The Basics With Four Hispanic Hotties

When I began to imagine what my first interview should entail, quite a few questions came rolling out of my brain. I knew that there were specific things that I wanted to get a girl's advice on (rather than my mom's, of course). So, I finally compiled a list of fundamental inquiries that I thought knowing the answers to would drastically advance the process of me, the chicken, aspiring to be the man my prospective wife will adore. I asked a young lady that I currently work with at Family Christian Stores, named Sylvia, to get some of her friends together so that I could interrogate them. Little did I know that they would end up teaching me so much about some seemingly trivial stuff.

I went to church the night of the interview to meet up with Sylvia and her three friends. Sylvia and I go to the same church, but I actually only met her a couple of months before this interview. I decided that we would go to Steak n' Shake, get some milkshakes, and start talking. When we got to the restaurant, there were a good number of college-age kids and adults populating the seats. The waitress seated us at a long table a peaceful distance from the clanging of dishes in the hectic kitchen.

The ladies present were Rebecka, Vicky, Sylvia, and Vanessa (Sylvia's sister). The first thing I noticed about the girls was the fact that they all seemed outgoing except for Vicky who was a bit more subdued. All of the beautiful young ladies were dressed fashionably. Sylvia was energized and ready to combat me at every turn. Rebecka had this really cool sense of humor. I could tell that she had the ability to take many of the problems associated with relationships with a dose of laughter. And Vanessa definitely added some 'older sister' wisdom to the table (even though she only appeared to be in her early twenties). Finally, Vicky . . . Well, Vicky didn't say much, but when she did, it was very compelling.

I am embarrassed to say that I didn't quite expect the girls to tell me anything I hadn't already come across. Needless to say, I was wrong. Once I got situated, I pulled my pen out, set my old Norwood tape recorder on the table, and let the questions fly.

Most of us Christian guys have a fairly similar ideal when it comes to the way a girl dresses. We definitely like to be attracted to a girl's body. Hey, there's nothing wrong with that. This attitude can be seen in the Bible. Isaac's son Jacob loved a woman named Rachel who was said to have a 'shapely figure' (Genesis 29:17). Since clothes pretty much sheathe a girl's figure a lot like the wrapping on a Christmas present, the way a girl dresses is a pretty important area for us guys.

Not that we really care about how our gifts are wrapped, but let's say for a second that you wanted to get a good idea of what the gift was before Christmas rolled around. Well, you certainly would want the wrapping to be somewhat form-fitting. The same goes for babes; we want to be able to somewhat discern the package. On the other hand, we wouldn't want our Christmas gift to be tossed under the tree in a transparent, plastic grocery bag. That would seem cheap and all the surprise would be gone with the first glance. In the same vein we don't want to be overly stimulated into lust by a girl revealing too much so it turns out to be a delicate matter. I wondered if these girls had any idea what guys tend to look for, so for the first question I asked, "How do you girls feel that guys want you to look?"

"It depends," Sylvia quickly replied. "There is a way that he wants his future wife to look and then there is a way that he wants the girl he dates to look. He wants the girl he dates to show a little so that he can get a little. Then he wants the girl he marries to be a little more reserved."

At this point I stopped to remind Sylvia that these are Christian guys we were talking about, thinking that she was talking about dudes that didn't know Jesus.

"No, but a lot of Christian guys are like that," she retorted.

It's kind of funny, but the more I thought about her statement, the more I realized it's pretty true. (Except for maybe the wife being reserved part.) The really misunderstood thing in Christian circles today is the fact that we shouldn't want our women hot. Don't get me wrong, I'm not talking "stripper sexy," but that old sentiment that beauty is on the inside is far overused. Yes, true beauty is what you'll find in the character of a person, but that doesn't negate the fact that we must be attracted to our spouse. I am positive that when God made Adam and Eve and told them "Be fruitful, and multiply," (Gen. 1:28, KJV) Adam was like, "Ohhhh, I can definitely do that!" Just look at the way Adam spoke when he first saw Eve. The

NLT Bible says, "'At last!' Adam exclaimed. 'She is part of my own flesh and bone!'" Now that sounds like a man that was pretty darn excited.

Maybe it was the fact that he had been naming animals all day, but I think Adam had the hots for Eve. None of us guys want a girl that shows everything to anyone she meets. On the other hand, we don't want a girl that is always wearing skirts to the floor. I think that most mature Christian men want a girl that is ravishing, while still maintaining modesty. "Well, can't the ravishing part lead to sexual desire and sin?" you ask. Sure, a girl looking that fine can lead to sexual desire, but sexual desire isn't evil in and of itself. Sexual desire can easily be grouped together with sin. That's only because it often leads to some devastating sins not because they are one and the same. In this respect, sexual desire is similar to anger. Neither one is wrong. It's what we do with them that can ultimately lead to great good or our own peril.

I'm sure you've heard, sometime in the recent past, that you shouldn't get angry. It was probably from the same, well-meaning folks that would tell you how horrific premarital sexual desire is. The truth is that both sexual desire and anger are super-powerful tools. The rationale for some people's dread of such things has to do with the fact that when a mighty tool is used wickedly, it makes a forcible firearm for evil.

Let's take a toothpick, for example. Kinda neat, if you want to look like a stud with it hanging between your lips when walking out of a diner. Other than that, it is a pretty weak utensil. Well, imagine if you tried to use it for amoral purposes. You wouldn't get very far trying to murder some New York street thug with a toothpick. Then again what if you used a more effective tool such as an axe with depraved intent? The result would be far greater destruction.

That's why you have to be careful when using such a potent tool as sexual desire. After all, you wouldn't let a toddler play with an axe. Just like there is certainly a right time to use an axe, if you are contemplating marriage, then you better be prepared to wield your sexual desire.

The way I see it, sexual desire is comparable to fire. Both have a powerful appetite and can be used for immense good (fire for heating and forging iron, cooking, warming bods, etc., and sexual desire for leading you to a girl that will fulfill your desires in marriage); however, they can both destroy us if not controlled.

Vanessa interrupted my thought process as she said, "Well, I think that guys want a hot wife too."

Darn tootin', I thought.

Sylvia replied, "Yeah, but the girl they marry is the girl that they got to know and respect. They don't want a girl that all their guy friends will look down on."

I decided to move on as I asked, "Do guys make you feel pressured to look good?"

There was a silence then a consensus of "No" and "Not really" along with Rebecka's, "I could give a rat's behind."

I instantly thought that was an odd reaction coming from a group of girls that were obviously dressed so well. I figured I'd give them time to explain as I paused, waiting for their reasoning.

Sylvia then chimed in, "I think I try to look good for myself. Actually, most girls try to look good in competition with other girls. Most competition comes in the form of your friends; not to say consciously competing with each other but like, 'Man, Becky looks good today and we are going to the mall, and look how I look. Now I have to go home and dress cute because I can't be walking around here looking scrubby and she's looking cute.' And we're not even thinking about guys."

The other girls seemed to agree with that statement.

"Insights into the women's world," I mused.

Sylvia laughed as she offered her reply. "Insights into the Puerto Rican women's world. Well, we are all Hispanics."

Nowadays, whenever I'm walking through the mall, or anywhere else where girls gather, I usually disregard most any of them because it's so hard to tell if they are Christians or not. I mean, all you can really notice while passing by these ladies is whether they are dressed scandalously or not. The problem is that there are a great percentage of the 'or nots' that still aren't Christians.

I knew that it is often hard to tell if a girl is a Christian just by the way she dresses. So I composed my next question to see if there are any other subtle giveaways. "How do you let guys know that you are a Christian?"

"The way you act should show you are a Christian," Vicky said in a subdued and calm voice.

"The way you dress should show you're a Christian too," Rebecka said to my surprise.

Vicky then clarified saying, "Yeah, that too. For example, with guys, if you are all over him and giving him that type of vibe, what type of Christian does that make you? A true Christian has respect for themselves."

Sylvia then made it a point to tell me that she was directly in front of Mr. Norwood (my recorder) so she might sound really loud. The fact was that she just talked really loudly.

I felt that I had touched enough on these more serious aspects for my first interview. I wanted to hit more of a variety of questions that had a lighter tone. I switched up my line of questioning. "How much does the way a guy smells mean to you?"

At this point the girls exploded and I thought we might get banned from Steak n' Shake. I heard a symphony of "Ohhh!!!" and "It means everything." I now began to realize that smell might be a tad more important than I had previously thought.

Rebecka stated that, "If he doesn't smell good, then he is not worth talking to. Because when a guy smells good it means he takes care of himself."

Sylvia began to add, "And that lets you know he'll . . ." as Rebecka joined her in concluding, "take care of you." It was weird to see how alike the girls' thought processes were. I began to feel like just maybe these girls could read my mind. Then my whole sexy, mysterious, reporter persona would be blown. It was comforting to see that I was not receiving answers all across the board, but rather their replies seemed to be in accord. Perhaps these questions would uncover the mysterious universal secrets of women. Ok, probably not.

Sylvia then expanded upon her previous answer. "But, also it's like a trademark of your man. So when you smell that, wherever you go it makes you remember him. All of the good things he did."

The girls told me that is why girls will have stuffed animals or t-shirts sprayed with their guy's cologne to take on trips, etc. I didn't even know this really happened outside of shows like Full House. The girls mentioned that they would wear a shirt with their man's scent on it over and over again.

I wanted to get a little more information on the unsuspected importance of smell so I asked, "What is the most important smell: clothes, cologne, breath?"

Rebecka replied with force, "If he has funky breath you don't want to be close to that."

That reminded me of this one old guy I knew. His name was Bill and he always looked like he was dirty. He was a hard working little fella, but Bill definitely could've used a change of clothes once in a while. He always wore the typical old man striped shirt and a half-plastic, greasy ball cap. The thing that made Bill seem fresh to me was the fact that he continually had good breath. Every time I saw him, his breath was delightful, but never overpowering. His trick? Well, old Bill had figured out that pushing a piece of gum to its limits had its benefits. You see, even after a piece of gum loses its flavor and seems to be obsolete, don't pitch the wee chewable. Gum emits a soft smell that is almost undetectable to the user. However it's refreshing to every passerby even after it becomes tasteless. I have found that taking one stick of gum into public places can be a lifesaver. Just tear off a quarter stick and nibble it for pleasing exhalation.

Vanessa continued on as she said, "Well, I think that body odor is a big thing, because if they have cologne on but they have bad breath, sometimes the cologne over does the breath."

"No! If those guys try to whisper in your face you just want to throw up," Rebecka retorted.

The girls then said something about a certain person that they forced me to strike from the record.

Now that I had recognized the magnitude of smelling good I

was ready to move forward. "Okay, I've heard enough about stinky guys. What was the best compliment that you girls ever got from a guy?"

After this question sunk in, Sylvia immediately said she had two examples, but couldn't seem to remember either of them. Luckily, after a minute, the compliments popped back into Sylvia's head.

Sylvia stated, "I had a guy tell me that I was a woman of God. There are two things that a woman wants to hear. That she is a woman of God and that she is desired. Every woman wants to be beautiful and desired." Sylvia then persisted to tell me that the guy who gave her that compliment wasn't around anymore so I should erase that from the manuscript. (I guess compliments aren't everything.)

Vanessa said, "There was this part in this card my boyfriend gave me. It said he was watering the garden last week and he came across these beautiful, pink roses. He said that as beautiful as these pink roses were they could not compare to my beauty. Then he said I was like a rose and he's so lucky because he has the most beautiful flower in the whole world."

I know that a compliment like that sounds really corny but they are vital nonetheless. Most of the time us guys don't feel the need to voice how we feel. "No need to tell my dad I love him. He knows I love him." I could easily trick myself into falling for that load of garbage. But no matter what we know about ourselves, it is always nice and reassuring to hear it.

Just recently I took some of the drawings I was doing for this book to a couple of girls I had interviewed. Before I even presented the drawings to the girls I knew I was a good artist. Even though I grasped the fact that I was skillful at drawing, when the girls began to gather around me at church lavishing me with compliments it made all the difference in the world.

God knows that this is the way it works. Look what He did for Jesus. In the beginning of the seventeenth chapter of Matthew, Jesus took Peter, James and John up on a mountain. While they were there Jesus turned a dazzling white and Moses and Elijah appeared next to him. A moment after that, God spoke from a glorious cloud saying, "This is my beloved Son, and I am fully pleased with him," (v. 5). Now, Jesus knew that he was without sin, as he later challenged the Pharisees to accuse him of any wrongdoing. He knew he was pleasing to his Father. He knew his Father loved him without measure. Still, I guarantee you that Jesus loved to hear his Father's compliment even though he already knew it was true.

Take God's example and give compliments even when you feel the girls might already know how you feel.

I was glad to hear of some instances of inspiring compliments, but I wanted to know if there was a downside to it all. I asked the girls, "Have you ever had a bad compliment?"

"Yeah. Well, they meant it in a good way, but I took it the wrong way. They told me I had very nice, child-bearing hips," Rebecka told me.

Ouch! I would've commented on that, but Sylvia took care of business as she spurted out, "I would be like, what did you mean by that? I'm not bearing any of your children!"

In my past experience I have had a couple of occurrences where girls complimented me because they liked me, but they just weren't appealing to me. It didn't seem like a big deal to me because I was on the good side of things. The trouble comes when I think about giving a girl some flattering words, but I'm scared she'll find me repulsive.

In order to find out how girls managed such a situation, I inquired, "How do you handle a compliment from a guy that you aren't attracted to?"

In a Mary Poppins-pitched voice, Sylvia said, "I say, 'Thank you. That was very nice.'"

"Thanks, and your shirt's really cute too," Rebecka added in a humorous tone.

Vanessa then explained, "You are polite, but it's dry behind it, and there is no chemistry or flirtation."

So that's what all of those girls were doing to me!

Sylvia then peered at Vicky and said, "So Vicky, what about you? Stop eating fries for a second."

"Yeah, give it up, Vick," I said without thinking. After I said that I was thinking, *Oh crap, I just called this pretty girl a man's name.*

Fortunately, Sylvia quickly chimed in, "Awww. He called you Vick. Like me." (Whew! I was safe.)

Vicky swallowed her food and answered, "I don't know, I think I would just say 'Thank you.'"

The key that I learned from this part of the discussion was to take a hint. Some girls can't hold back their enthusiasm when it comes to you smooth-talking them. They will flirt back to let you know they're interested. Needless to say, that doesn't happen a lot with me. Other girls are more discreet and want you to work at luring them in. Then there are the girls that don't want you to hit on them and they're serious. When they cut the conversation short it's because they don't want to talk to you anymore. When that happens don't think, "I'm ugly and stupid! I knew she'd never like me." Just know that that girl was not as good for you as the one you're going to meet. The girl God intends for you will be extremely attracted to you.

Recently, my friend has been dealing with this very problem. He's a good looking guy that has a lot going for him, but three girls in a row have given him the 'cold shoulder' as soon as he tried to pursue anything more than friendship. I told him, "Don't worry. You're narrowing it down." He then told me in a defeated voice, "I've narrowed it down to zero, dude."

Sometimes we all feel like there are no options left. A lot of times this happens in areas far more critical than dating. Fear not! God often does His most miraculous work when we have nowhere else to turn.

As for flirting, here's the surprise; it's not evil. There is nothing more pure than letting a girl know you like her by paying special attention to her (i.e. by flirting). Just keep two things in mind while winking at the ladies. First, don't flirt unless you really are interested in knowing her as a wife. For example, don't rub a girl's arm just because she's hot even though you can't see it going any farther than playful touching. Unchecked flirting leads to a habit that will cause you big problems later. Second, don't bruise your conscience. Don't ever flirt to the point where you feel like you're being sinful. This means that MTV lap dances aren't considered godly flirtation. Stick to the 'complimenting-her-ring–while-lightly-holding–her-hand' kind of stuff.

The next pair of questions stemmed from my observations as a guy. So many times I would be walking in the mall and catch a glance of this super dorky guy with his arm wrapped around an impressive-looking girl. This seemed to be the case way more than it was a so-so woman with a studly guy. It got me wondering.

A short while ago I finally pieced the mystery together with help from my buddy, Johnny. Johnny is this really confident guy who is pretty decent looking, but he definitely won't be making it into 'GQ' anytime soon. (Johnny, if you're reading this, I'm talking about a different Johnny. Really!) Remarkably, Johnny has a darn hot wife. After probing all of Johnny's mannerisms, I discovered that he has a genuine sense of confidence about himself that shines through on a regular basis.

I've had a problem with gaining confidence for a long while now. When I first accepted Jesus as my savior I embraced a low self-image of myself, thinking that it was actually some form of humbleness. Truth be told, a humble view of oneself will never see you as less than you really are.

I have had to learn (often slowly) the importance of having a confident outlook about myself and my relationship with Christ. Since confidence is a valuable but scarce commodity for me, I wanted to check what it meant to the ladies, so I inquired, "How much does a guy's confidence mean to you?"

"If he is overconfident, it's unattractive," Rebecka answered with a tad bit of disgust to her voice.

Vicky continued, "Because then it's all about themselves and then they forget about you. They should be giving you some attention."

I wasn't exactly expecting the girls to comment on the flip side of confidence. In fact, when a guy acts like that, self-absorbed and overly confident, it's really the confidence imposter, pride, spurring him on. Just as I misread low self-esteem to be humbleness, so pride can be mistaken for confidence.

That reminded me of something important. You know when you are out with a group of people and you always want to be confident so that everybody notices you and laughs at your jokes? Well, think about it the other way around for a second. What do you think about the loudmouth person soaking up all of the attention? You probably wish they would share a little of the spotlight and show some interest in you. That would make you feel good. Remember that emotion when you are feeling like the 'pimp daddy' and all eyes are on you. Everybody else is probably not feeling as good as you are and it might be time to spread the joy by focusing on someone else.

At this point in the interview the women still weren't done bashing arrogant guys.

"And sometimes their confidence is confidence in their manhood and they end up being some sexist jerk that I want to smack," Sylvia continued with flair.

Whoa! Remind me never to do my Fonzie impression in front of Sylvia.

"I like a guy that can joke around about himself," Vanessa voiced.

Sylvia then stated, "But I do like confident guys because if they're insecure, the whole relationship is going to go . . . ."

At that point the waiter broke up the conversation to check on us. I mentioned to the young women how I really wished I had picked up the ability to write in shorthand somewhere along the way. I never knew it would be so hard to keep up with four fast-talking ladies. Good thing I had Mr. Norwood.

Soon enough the waiter departed from our company, although he did seem vaguely interested in what we were talking about (as did the rest of the restaurant).

Ok, here was the question to see if us guys have a chance of finding a hotter babe than we deserve. "Can a guy's confidence ever overshadow his looks?" I implored.

From this question I got, in unison, "definitely," "definitely," "definitely," and a more cynical "let me pray about it," from Rebecka.

Vanessa presented evidence for the case at hand by saying, "The guy that I'm with right now, I mean he's really, really cute, but he's not the kind of guy that I would see walking in the mall and be like, 'Oh my gosh!'"

Rebecka scrutinized her answer by asking, "But was it his confidence or personality?"

Vanessa held fast to her point asserting, "His personality and his confidence. Because he's confident in who he is and that reflects in his personality."

Rebecka receded as she noted, "I haven't come across that yet."

Sylvia affirmed Vanessa's claim by saying, "Oh, I have."

Rebecka then sought after proof as she made the demand, "Tell me one . . . ."

The girls all began to whisper in secrecy. Next book, I will be getting myself voice taps to stick under the chairs of the people I'm interviewing.

Overall, I was pleased to hear the girls' conclusions on that last question. It certainly seemed as though a guy's self-confidence could sway the vote when it came to catching a woman's heart.

Ever since I used to hit the malls, hunting down pretty, junior-high babes (Yes, I was in junior high too) I've had a lack of style in the fashion department. Maybe it was due to the fact that I've got some awkward color blindness that makes it so I can't tell the difference between dark greens and blacks. Or maybe it's because I've got no fashion sense. Whatever the case, I learned from the Christmas season to always wear the clothes my sister got me. I didn't know they were stylish while I was holding them dangling above a freshly torn package, but I always found out later. I wanted to get the inside scoop on a guy's apparel, so I asked, "How important is it that a guy dresses nicely?"

Again, there was an eruption of "yes" and "yup."

Vanessa remarked, "If they don't and you fall for them, you make them dress nice anyway."

"Yeah, you sure do. You change the way they dress. To change their style to what you want your man to have," Rebecka explained.

"Most guys don't care so it's not that big of a deal," Vanessa pointed out.

True. I'd dress like a clown selling corn dogs to get a babe.

I examined the issue further. "What is dressing nicely? Like staying in style?"

The girls voiced a group "yeah."

"Wearing clothes that fit and are not too big," Rebecka clarified.

I knew that Rebecka's comment had hit something crucial. Most girls that I have come in contact with like to see a guy in clothes that fit. They want to be able to make out your figure, so no thirty-inch pant legs on your jeans. Then again, girls don't like to be able to read the brand of your boxer briefs through your jeans. So if that's you, loosen em' up a little, cowboy.

Vanessa continued, "Also, dressing like yourself. I would

never put Carson" (I assumed this was her man) "in all 'Express' because he's a country boy. But he looks great in 'Abercrombie and Fitch' and 'American Eagle.'" She then stated that a guy should, "Try not to be somebody he is not for somebody he is with."

"Right, right," Rebecka agreed.

There went the 'clown-dog' costume. I knew that what the girls were saying here sounded a little contradictory, but let me explain it the way I understood their view. They want to mold the way you dress into Studdom, yet they don't want you to be someone you truly aren't just for them. I think the point was that girls have a superior fashion sense and know better than you do what you look good in. Even so, they don't want you to alter your whole demeanor just for the sake of the clothes.

At this point, Sylvia kept peeking at my list of questions and I had to give her a stern warning.

I have known for quite some time that women don't look at men the same way guys look at women. Any guy could tell you that a woman's body is an extremely attractive sight. Us guys have to really battle with our eyes in order to stay holy. Sometimes that requires staring straight at the ground whether it be to avoid a grocery store 'gossip mag' or a woman in a provocative skirt. Well, it's not quite the same for ladies.

Women are repulsed by a lot of our hairy, sweaty parts. More often than not, they find a man fully clothed more stimulating than if he were undressed. It's just a plain fact that women are more turned on by attitude than we are. I didn't know what type of answer I would get regarding my next question, but I had to find out. "Ok, ladies, on this question be serious and don't just give me the Christian, politically correct answer. What's the bigger draw: looks or attitude?"

The girls wanted me to elaborate on my question. I explained that if there were two guys, one that was moderately attractive but had a great attitude and another that was gorgeous, but had a crappy attitude, which one would they pick? They all seemed to agree on the guy with the better attitude.

Sylvia declared, "I don't have a specific type of guy when it comes to looks, but I do have a specific when it comes to attitude and personality."

I didn't know if the girls were being honest with me or if they were answering the way they thought they should. Nonetheless, it was still pretty cool to hear because I can work on my attitude, but for the most part, I'm stuck with the way I look.

I persisted to quiz the girls on the subject of attitude. "What is the best attitude for a guy to have?"

"Easygoing," Vanessa said softly.

Rebecka expressed her earlier loathing of overconfident guys, as she said, "Not conceited. That is so unattractive. I just want to 'pop' them."

Sylvia mentioned, "That's like the biggest thing. They have to be able to make me laugh."

"Sometimes shy is cute, but sometimes it's not. If they are too quiet it's like, 'Oh, please just talk already,'" Rebecka established.

I then coerced Vicky to answer by requesting her opinion.

"Ummmm, what was the question?" Vicky uttered gently.

I explained that I wanted to know what the best attitude for a guy to have was.

Vicky answered, "My favorite attitude would have to be somebody that I can joke with. I want somebody that knows when's the right time to joke and when's the right time to be serious too. I think that's very important because there are times when you could be talking about something and they just keep joking about it and you're trying to be serious and you're like 'Rrrrrrrr' [*some sort of animal noise*]. You just get frustrated."

"Very good point," Rebecka confirmed.

That was definitely a good point. A lot of times we guys want so badly to make the girls laugh that we don't know when to stop. Did you ever see 'Beauty and the Geek' on TV? It was the reality show where they put a bunch of super-smart, nerdy guys with a group of hot, not-so-smart babes. Vicky's insight reminded me of Richard, one of the geeks on the first season who made it all the way to the final episode. Richard made me laugh quite a bit, but that's only because he never ceased trying to be funny. Odds were that if he made a million jokes a day, I was bound to laugh at a few of them. I spent the rest of the time being annoyed.

Obviously, girls like a guy with a good sense of humor, as they've been saying. But a good sense of humor entails a shut-off valve. Just like Solomon said, "Too much honey will make you sick".

My next question stemmed from my mall-bopping days. When I was a young, hormone-heavy teen, I used to head out to the mall and go on the prowl. My friends and I would hunt down any cute-looking schoolgirl and send out some animalistic vibes. The kind of vibes that said, "Hey, I like you 'cause you're hot."

Things have changed. When I now look for a girl, I have to

know she's a Christian. Not just a girl that believes God made all of the fuzzy creatures, but a woman that recognizes Jesus Christ as her Lord and Savior. I figured these ladies had similar requirements for the guys they check out. So I asked, "How do you know that a guy knows Jesus?"

"Personally, and this is going to sound so bad," Rebecka admitted. "And there is not always a situation where you can hear it: I will know if I'm going to like a guy or not by the way he prays."

Sylvia said, "A good way is, when you're going on a date, have him pray for the food."

Actually, that didn't sound weird to me at all. Think about a little bratty kid in the grocery store. How do you know he's a brat? Usually by the way he talks to his parents. The problem is that guys are usually a little less conspicuous than a five-year-old sitting by the frozen foods screaming because he can't have a Popsicle. Still, why not check out a guy's character by observing the way he talks to his Dad? (And if you were wondering, the answer is yes. I did hold my breath until my face turned blue in the grocery store as a practical joke on my mom when I was real little. Oh, you weren't wondering?!)

There are two ways I can think of to tell a guy doesn't have a good relationship with his spiritual father through prayer. First, if the guy does some proper and practiced, melodramatic prayer, then you know something's fishy. Kind of like when you see a little kid acting so sweet to her parents that it makes you sick. When people have a tone of flattery behind their words it's usually because they have ulterior motives. Of course God sees right through that crap and most godly women probably do too.

CHRISTIAN BABE ALERT

Second, when a guy prays, if he sounds uneasy and nervous about the language he uses with God it could just be because there's a hot girl listening to him or, more likely it could be, because he hasn't done it in a while.

Take a teenage boy who hasn't spoken to his biological dad for a while. Say that the kid's dad left him and his mother when he was still a baby. If he suddenly gets that out of the blue phone call from his dad, chances are the conversation wouldn't be bustling with activity. It would doubtless be filled with long pauses and dry, heartless speech. I'm not telling you guys to practice praying in a manner that will trick the girls into liking you. I'm saying: spend some time each day talking to your Father in Heaven. After a short while, your prayers will be as natural as asking your mom for money. I know it's not as easy to talk to God because he's not there in a tangible way like your parents, but always know that He will spend any time you want to listen to you.

After getting a great answer for my previous question I was moving on. "What is the best way for a guy to let you know he's interested in you?"

Sylvia began to give me some pointers to consider while on a group date. She said how guys should, "make the effort to sit next to you, and to find out more about you." She then proclaimed, "Girls don't want pickup lines. They want conversation. They want to get to know the person."

I found her last comment really amusing. In every romantic comedy I've ever seen, the guys who are good with the ladies always had about twenty, sure-fire pickup lines up their sleeves. Take James Bond, for example. He always seemed so suave as he tossed out one-liners that made the women melt like butter.

The funny thing is that us guys pay too much heed to such movies. Expecting to get a girl with a pick-up line is like counting on catching a lion with a piece of cheese. Yes, that cheese may draw the lion in, but you sure better have a cage to trap him or he'll eat you alive. Our so-called 'cage' is known as conversation. (Around this point in my train of thought I realized I would have to do an interview that was more devoted to conversing with women. Check out my last interview with Stephanie and Amy to get a deeper look at utilizing conversation time.)

Sylvia then added one more touch a guy could apply to show his interest. "Then he can subtly find a reason to get your number," she said.

After I was done thinking about girls wanting conversation, we took a quick break for the girls to rip on my huge and ugly writing. Rebecka actually said, "Awww, he does have big writing," almost as if I had 20-inch deformed ears.

Since Sylvia brought up dating I thought I'd ask, "For a first date, group or not, where would a good place be?"

At that point the girls mentioned a couple of places like the beach or bowling alley, but I found it even more fascinating where Rebecka said not to go. "Don't go to the movie theater for a first date." Us guys love movies and having a beautiful girl on our arm is even better. Unfortunately, the movies pretty much neutralize all dialogue that should've been present. A first date should give you plenty of time to talk to each other. (More on that topic later.)

Okay, I knew I was getting a ton of information and my brain couldn't hold much more, but there was one question I was dying to ask. This question was a little off topic, but it seemed to fit in with this first, free-for-all style interview.

I'm one of those guys that wouldn't mind my wife staying at home to raise the kids even if it meant we would have to live on a lot less. I'd actually prefer it that way. The trouble is that almost as many women as men are pursuing careers these days. I think it has a lot to do with the fact that men have done a typically crappy job of supporting women. Many men, especially in the recent past, have left their women with the babies they helped create, but with no means to support them. It seems women have taken the initiative to make sure it doesn't happen anymore. I wanted to know what these sharp, young ladies thought about the matter. "What if a guy wants to be the sole supporter and wants you to watch the kids," I probed.

Rebecka immediately responded, "My attitude on that, like, as for myself, right now I'm in college and I'm pursuing a career. I don't want to feel like I wasted my time. I did not go to school all these years to marry someone then have them say, 'Oh well, I want you to stay home with the kids.' Well, I guess we are not having kids anytime soon."

Wow! That answer was definitely more drastic than I had planned for. So there was only one thing I could say. "But you have such good child bearing hips!" (Just kidding, I didn't say that.) All joking aside, Rebecka's response threw me for a loop and I wondered if the other girls felt the same.

Vicky confirmed my fears as she said, "I need to think about the future. God forbid, if something were to happen to my husband. I need to be able to support my kids. I need to have my education. I need to have a career. You want to make sure that your kids are still going to have a comfortable life. I went through a lot when I was younger. It was my mother alone, and she didn't have that background. She didn't have that education. So I don't care what my husband says, because I want to make sure I can support my children."

The girls all did agree that some women believe it is their ministry to raise children up in a godly way and they really respected that. The girls told me that men should seek such women out if that is what they desired. That kind of put me in a rough spot. Fortunately, I knew that God would indeed lead me to a woman that felt the need to raise up godly children.

I knew that the interview was drawing to a close as the girls had pretty much slurped their milkshakes dry. One last thing I wanted to cover before we left was summed up as I said, "What is one thing that you would tell guys to do differently?"

"In any area?" Vanessa quizzed.

"Anything. Anything that bugs you about men," I said.

Vanessa was ready to respond as soon as I finished talking. "I think . . . Okay, I've got one. This is just something that I've noticed. Maybe I would change their mindset to realize that a girl is a lot different than a guy. So in a lot of things, my boyfriend tends to treat me or girls around him the way he would treat his brothers and his guy friends. You have to realize that girls are different. So their needs are different, their emotions are different, the way they carry themselves is different, and their topics of conversation are different. You just have to be sensitive to that. You know what I mean? The way you joke around. You just need to be aware. I would change that about guys."

I guess that means no more hitting my sister. Seriously though, 'guys and girls being different' is the main theme of this book. If girls were like guys I wouldn't need to ask them millions of questions in order to better relate to them. Since women are so distinct, it is of vital importance that us guys approach them with some foreknowledge of these distinctions.

"I think too, this is gonna sound stupid," Rebecka said with a smile, "but every girl wants that Prince Charming, and if a guy's not romantic you don't feel like you're something to be caught."

"Exactly!" Sylvia added with emphasis. "Don't get too comfortable in the relationship to the point where you stop romanticizing them because the girl is going to get bored and she's not going to feel like she's loved anymore."

My brain took a swift pause to contemplate whether or not romanticizing was an actual word. Later, I looked it up and it turned out that it was. Who would have thunk it?

"You might just think," Sylvia continued, "'Oh, well we just got to that point in our relationship now and I don't have to do those things because I have her.' That's not the truth, because, don't think that until the ring's on her finger."

"No, and even afterwards . . .," concluded Rebecka.

Sylvia then showed some unexpected affection for my tape recorder as she spouted out, "It's ok, Norwood! I love you!" She then proceeded to add to her answer as she said, "I like a guy that has confidence. But, like I said about the pride issue, when it gets to the point that they have so much pride they feel like you can't help them 'cause they want to handle things on their own—or they don't go to a Christian mentor—when pride gets in the way it can destroy a relationship. So guys need to check their pride, often-times. That's something I think a lot of guys deal with. Even Christian guys. Especially Christian guys, because they think that they can handle everything on their own because they are 'Mr. Man-of-God' or something."

"Or even just weaknesses they have," Rebecka tacked on.

"Exactly," corroborated Sylvia.

Rebecka resolved, "Everybody has weaknesses."

What!? Like us guys 'think' we can handle it all. We *know* we can handle it all. That can certainly be a problem sometimes. Instead of thinking we can handle it all, we need to know our limits. I once read somewhere that being humble means, "Knowing exactly what you can do and nothing more." When we have a reasonable image of what we can and cannot do, it makes for an easy time in being both humble and confident. The predicament us guys often fall into occurs when we attempt more than we think we can handle. I'm not talking about 'Moses-parting-the-Red-Sea' kind of more than a man can handle. That circumstance involved God managing an impossible situation. I'm speaking of 'a-guy-carrying-one-too-many-12-packs-of-Pepsi-to-the-picnic-table' kind of more than a man can handle. I once tried to carry so many blue, plastic grocery bags full of food into the house that my fingers went numb for a week.

Yes, all of us young guys want to be strong. Solomon noticed this in Proverbs 20:29 when he stated, "The glory of the young is their strength; the gray hair of experience is the splendor of the old." Luckily, some of us were born with supernatural might (cough). Although there is actually something more important than strength. When Solomon chronicled the 'gray hair of experience' he wasn't pointing out the drawbacks of men's hair coloring. He was saying that mature, typically older men value their wisdom over their strength. Aged men don't hold wisdom in higher esteem only because they're commonly scrawny and weak. Rather because, as Solomon so candidly put it, "Wisdom is mightier than strength," (Proverbs 24:5, The Living Bible).

What is all of this nonsense about wisdom and strength? Let me put it this way: I can guarantee that a woman wants you to be strong (or able to handle certain situations), but you will never appear that way without wisdom. I'll give you a quick example of strength without wisdom, or as Sylvia put it, "the pride issue."

One time, my dad, who is a tough, Italian mechanic, decided to visit the gym that his buddy had invited him to. When he got there, he proceeded to lift more weights than he should have in an attempt to impress his friends. Consequently, he came home and threw up.

We've all been there. Trying to act manly at the cost of some of our better judgment. Unfortunately, as Sylvia mentioned, ladies don't want an act. It's a good thing that God has endowed in each of us an undeniable, masculine intensity. The key is to use it without overusing it. Don't ever think that you're too good for another person's help, especially your soon-to-be wife.

While I'm on this rampage of advice, here is one more nugget of critical counsel. Being strong is not always physical. My dad would have been stronger if he had told his friends he didn't want to try to lift that much weight. A lot of times my dad actually hurt my mom because he was too weak to put her first. You see, my dad was strong enough to beat a lot of other guys up and in this world that's toughness. On the other hand, my dad was too weak to tell people he had to leave early because he had promised my mom he would go out with her. To

God, your toughness is defined by your will, not your fists. For example, look at the story of Joshua in the Bible. He was a beast of a fighter, conquering just about every humanoid that stood in his way. Joshua wasn't able to do that because he studied 'Ultimate Fighting' secrets. He did it because he was determined to follow God's will, regardless of how scared he was. If you don't think Joshua was afraid, notice how God had to tell him not to be fearful right from the start (Joshua 1:9).

As a crazy side note; just before I read this chapter of my book today, giving it a little touch-up, my mom had called me and told me that although I may feel like my girl might be impressed with me physically fighting for her (I'm having some problems with a tough guy neighbor at the moment), that's not what girls really want. No matter how counter-intuitive this seems to my masculine ego it keeps proving itself true to me. Women genuinely want us to be strong in the character department more so than in the body type, as corny as it sounds. They want us to choose their side over our friends and parents. They want us to be able to say "no" when necessary.

We as men will have many opportunities to say no to others for the sake of our wives. Trust me when I say that, at times, it might even be scary to take your wife's side. Especially when you face the thought of making your friends mad or even the reality of losing a job. This is where true strength comes into play. My brother-in-law, Tom, is a prime example. He is almost always willing to face me and my cousins' wrath when he says he can't do something with us because he wants to spend time with his wife. That's not easy to make people unhappy, but he knows that his main obligation lies with his wife.

After I gathered a few more tidbits that can be found in the

"Babe Talk" sections, I said my good-byes to the ladies and headed home. As I coasted home on the cool, black road, streetlights glowing through my windshield, I contemplated all I had heard. I was amazed to think that I had learned so much about the way women feel from such simple questions. I was really impressed with the depth of knowledge these women exhibited and was anxious to get on with more interviews. From only one interview, my brain was buzzing and I knew that Norwood was sweating from an overload of information. I didn't know how much more of this good stuff my old buddy could handle.

There was actually a funny follow-up to this interview. A few weeks after I had interviewed Sylvia, I was working with her at the Family Christian Store doing inventory. It was us and about ten other employees putting in some late night hours in order to count all of the store's stock. One of the other workers was none other than my sister. I figured I'd tell this story in order to display how much I truly need the advice these girls impart in such interviews.

I had informed Sylvia that I needed to talk to her about something before she left and told her to remind me. A little after midnight as Sylvia popped open the back door to our store to leave, she remembered what I had said. She was holding open our massive rear door that leads to the mall parking lot as she turned to me and asked what I had wanted. I told her that I needed to sketch her caricature for the book, but since it was so late I'd do it another time. She then proceeded to say, "Well, do you want to walk me to my car?"

I thought for a millisecond and then replied, "No thanks, I can't draw you while we're walking out there."

At that point my sister, who would've probably smacked me had she been closer, cried out, "She's scared, you retard!"

After my long walk across the deserted parking lot to Sylvia's car and back, I received a little more sisterly compassion. As soon as I cracked the back door she said, "Oh my gosh! You are so oblivious. How are you ever going to get a girl?"

As stupid as I may have seemed, I definitely learned to be more outgoing with women. Just because I might not be captivated by a girl doesn't mean I can't get some gentleman-like practice.

I later told my chum Gary about what my sister had said, and my overall obliviousness to Sylvia's request. He echoed, "Well, either I've never had any moments like that with girls, or I've been oblivious to them all!"

Interview Dos (2)

Two Staggering Beauties Tell Me All About Romance

Babe Talk
Which Body Part?
When 20 girls were required to reveal which male body part they were more attracted to, arms, chest or stomach:
60% answered arms,
20% said chest,
and 20% were drawn in by the tight abs.
"All of it! Whatever they'll show me!" *—Faith*

Two Staggering Beauties Tell Me All About Romance

I felt like it was time to get the lowdown on the softer side of gentlemen. I figured that there was no better young lady to quiz than the girl that first caught my eye when I started going to my present church. She is actually a little babe that sings on the praise team named Selina. (I talk pretty big for a guy that rarely even speaks to girls I find attractive, huh? I'm writing so it's easy.) Selina brought her friend, Faith, to the interview. Faith just so happens to be another cutie that sings with her. I decided to take these two young ladies to Applebee's for some discussion while dining.

This interview was a little more intimidating than the one before it was, due to the fact that these girls seemed to know everyone. When we first arrived at Applebee's, it almost appeared to be a family reunion night for the girls. They waved and laughed and said "hello" to all kinds of people before we got seated. It made me feel like I was interviewing two movie stars. After a minute into the interview, I was far more comfortable as I realized that these two ladies were very down-to-earth and just as excited as I was to be there.

The booths surrounding us were filled with conversation

and cheer. The place was packed. As soon as our waitress took our drink orders, I settled into the vinyl seat and focused my attention on the two ladies.

I decided to do an interview on romance because I kind of view it like a woman's 'sex.' I know that sounds stupid to a man's ears, but let me explain. All of you male readers know that sex is our goal. Yes, we desire all of the mushy times of cuddling by the fireplace, but let's not kid ourselves; we want it to lead to sex.

There is nothing wrong with that. If there were, it would be a pretty sparsely populated Earth. The problem is that women aren't quite like us in this respect. They could just as easily have a wonderfully romantic day with you and fall asleep next to you after a long stimulating conversation without ever wanting sex. Crazy, huh?

Women want romance like we want sex. And I'm not talking about giving her flowers after you get home from work so you can have sex. I'm talking about making your wife a priority all day long without the guarantee of sexual gratification later. We sell a book at the bookstore where I work that has a title that sums it all up. It's called "Sex begins in the Kitchen."

If you're asking yourself how knowing this will help you find your Christian babe, stay with me for a minute. Just as you would search for a woman that looks sexually appealing to be your wife, women search for a man who is romantically inclined even before marriage. In theory, if we learn what being romantic means to women, we can adjust ourselves accordingly.

Sadly, this interview was interrupted when I recognized the fact that Norwood, my 1902 tape recorder, had cut out midway through the conversation. (In all fairness I think it was my fault. Ok, ok, so I pressed the wrong button!) So I had to do a little more legwork, calling the ladies at home, to complete the interview. Besides that hiccup, the interview was a blazing success. Faith turned out to be a fireball with a quick, comedic wit and Selina won my heart with her sincere, experienced answers. So, get ready for the inside scoop on romance.

As I started the interview, the first thing that popped into my brain was the fact that I wanted this book to be as realistic a representation of Christian women as I could get. I knew that some of the questions I was going to ask could easily receive an 'approved of' answer that was different than what these young women really felt inside. Kind of like in a job interview when they ask you, 'Do you ever get angry at fellow employees?' The recommended reply would be to tell them, 'Oh no! I never get angry.' Everyone knows it's a lie, but that's what they want to hear. That may be a tad exaggerated, but we all know we sometimes tend to talk in a way that we feel we are expected to talk. Well, I wanted to hear that these girls do get angry. I wanted to know how they really felt. This was my only chance at getting answers that would shape me into the man I needed to become.

"Ok," I began, "I'm going to ask you these questions. Just answer them as honestly as you can, and don't try to give me the "Christian answer" that you think I want to hear."

"Now that he said it, ok!" Faith said with an exaggerated sigh of relief.

Selina laughed at Faith's response.

I figured I'd get right to the point as I said, "First one is:

how important is it to you girls that guys are romantic?"

Selina paused for a good five seconds before she asked with firm curiosity, "How do you want us to answer that?"

"I think it's important," Faith began, before I could explain to Selina, "because, even though I don't come from a really romantic family—like my parents are not really romantic with each other—I think it shows effort on the guy's part. Even if I don't always receive it well, the fact that they are going out of their way to be romantic shows that, 'Ok, I must be important to them.' But then there's a down side to that because romance can also be used to entice a girl . . ."

"Manipulate," Selina integrated.

"Yeah, it can be used as a manipulative thing as well," continued Faith.

"Good," I said as I turned to Selina. "That's how you answer it."

"Uh huh, yeah, ok," Selina replied in a sweet, accepting tone.

I joked with the girls as I said, "Man, you just took like five of my questions, what the heck are you doing?"

"Oh, I'm sorry," Faith uttered.

"I'm just kidding," I said as I prepared to ask my next question. "To you ladies, what does the word 'romance' mean? What does it entail?"

Faith boldly told me, "I don't do definitions."

Selina agreed as she stated, "I know." Then Selina searched her mind for an interpretation. "What does it mean? I think romance is just like a . . . It's probably more like a passion. A passion with an intimacy. Because, for you to be romantic with somebody, you have to be passionately in love with them. And for you to be passionately in love with them, there has to be some level of intimacy," she said.

When you first read Selina's answer you might think it's a little too deep. I mean, we can be romantic without all of those absorbing feelings, right? Well, the more you ponder it, the more you'll realize that, right from the start, girls see romance as something more involved than we usually do. Guys initially think of romance as the things you do to get a girl to like you, but although such romantic gestures are key to initiating any relationship, they are only the gel icing on the Dairy Queen ice cream cake. Selina immediately pointed out that romance goes a lot farther than opening the car door and is actually the result of passion and intimacy.

It kind of reminded me of Paul and James' little dispute in the Bible. In Romans 3, Paul says that we are saved by faith alone and our salvation is not based on our deeds. But then James states, in James 2:17 that it isn't enough to just have faith and that faith without good deeds is dead. Amazingly, the two statements fit together perfectly. Paul is telling us that true faith in Jesus Christ results in salvation. Then James explains to us what true faith is. James shows the characteristic of true faith to bear good deeds. Kind of like if you went into a truck stop bathroom and didn't see any urinals, you would know it wasn't the guys' restroom. The urinals are a sign that the restroom is for guys. The fact that you saw no urinals is evidence that this is not the guys' restroom. So it is with a person who says they have faith but never presents any good deeds. You know it's not genuine faith because such faith is never without good deeds. James just differentiated between the kind of faith that Paul was talking about (one that doesn't require good deeds to attain salvation but rather invariably produces them) from the counterfeit faith that can't save anyone.

I know . . . I know . . . That was pretty complex and you're thinking, 'This dude's crazy. What the heck did that have to do with romance?' Well, I think that Selina kind of exemplified the fact that authentic romance comes as an outcome of an intimate passion for someone just like good works come by means of real faith. That's all I was trying to say . . . Geez . . . I hope you learned something, you bunch of impatient, macho . . . Oh my gosh, these girls are rubbing off on me . . .

My biggest problem right now isn't that I'm not attracted to any women. I can think of a couple off the top of my head that I wouldn't mind taking a stroll down the 'lane of love' with. My issue is that I haven't felt God's direction towards any of the good-looking girls I've come across. Right now I think of it almost like I view helping poor people.

Have you ever come across a homeless person on the road and you suddenly got that churning feeling in your gut? The kind of burning sensation where you know you should do something? That has definitely happened to me before. But a lot of times I'll pass a poor person on the street with no inherent urge to help them. Does that make me a bad Christian? Of course not! I have to follow the Holy Spirit's leading in such instances or, within a short time, I'd be begging too. Don't get this confused with doing something God has instilled in you to do that seems like it will break your bank. Those investments never leave you broke. I'm saying, don't invest without advice. God gave us this wisdom way back in the eleventh century BC when He had Samuel say, "Obedience is far better than sacrifice (Samuel 15:22)." That means that it is more important to listen to God than it is to just do what we want to do for Him.

A quick example of this has to do with me cleaning the house. When I used to clean the house for my mom I often found myself doing what I enjoyed the most (or should I say hated the least.) I usually vacuumed or washed dishes, but I rarely ever dusted because I hate dusting. I mean, you've got to move every stinking object in order to swipe away millions of insignificant little particles that reappear seconds later. Now I could have very easily continued to do what I wanted to for my mom, and that would have been pretty cool. Or I could have done what she really wanted me to do, like tedious dusting, and that would have been far better. See the correlation? (Later in the week, after writing this, I actually took my own advice and did some stupid dusting.)

If we are willing, God will always give us the 'go ahead' when the time comes to do something. The necessary element is being sure you're ready. Don't say to God, 'Point me to a hungry person so that I can help,' if you really aren't prepared to do just that. James said it best in James 1:5. He wrote, "If you need wisdom—if you want to know what God wants you to do—ask him, and he will gladly tell you. He will not resent your asking. But when you ask him, be sure that you really expect him to answer, for a doubtful mind is as unsettled as a wave of the sea that is driven and tossed by the wind."

God showed me this in a situation where I wasn't ready. I was driving by the hospital one afternoon and I felt like praying for every sick person that was in there that day. (I'm such a good, Christian boy.) But, as I was waiting at the red light, perpendicular to the huge hospital, I got the push to go in: for what reason I will never know, because I was too much of a sissy to get out of my car. I wanted to pray for the hospital, but I was not willing to be obedient for anything more.

Okay, to the point before I tell you my whole life story. I know, as I said earlier, that I need to go where godly women are. While I'm there I expect that God will give me that same upside-down stomach feeling (in a good, roller coaster kind of way) that I get when I see a person I should help, when I do finally come across the right girl. The thing is that I need to be ready to take action when that happens. So I felt like I should get some good suggestions on how to approach my babe when I find her.

I said, "Ok, number three."

Faith gave me that inquisitive, child-like expression as she said, "Can we both answer a question? I'm just curious."

"Yeah! Yeah. Spit it out. Give me all the goods you got," I quipped. Then I asked, "What is a romantic way for a guy to let you know he's interested in you?"

Faith began, "Well, for girls and guys, there is different . . . what's that called . . . the five love languages." (Faith was talking about Gary Chapman's best-selling book entitled 'The Five Love Languages'. In the book Chapman made use of his skill as a marriage counselor to differentiate between the diverse ways people express and receive love. The five ways expounded upon in the book are: 'acts of service,' 'receiving gifts,' 'quality time,' 'physical touch,' and 'words of affirmation.') "And so it kind of depends on what you are." Faith gazed at Selina, anticipating a response as she continued, "I know you are like more of a what?"

Selina said, "I don't know, I didn't read it."

I laughed as I heard Selina's response.

Faith kept going as she said, "No, I mean there's buying gifts and there's . . ."

Selina broke Faith's concentration as she laughed out loud at Faith's persistent attempt to make her remember something she had never read.

"C'mon, we're on tape," Faith communicated in a flustered and whimsical tone.

Selina was still cracking up as she said, "I don't know."

Faith moved back to 'The Five Love Languages' to indicate the ways that a guy could best show his love for her. "So like for me, I'm like 'give me gifts.' That shows to me romance. Whereas some people would rather you do something for them to be romantic . . . I don't even think that is the question," she finished, not knowing if she had answered my initial inquest.

At that point I was a little unsure myself as to what I had asked. I had got caught up in these two girls shining their 'pearly whites' at me in a medley of giggles. I knew I couldn't let these two beauties pull me in like a duet of sirens. So I quickly reconfigured my attitude to that of a hardened journalist as I said, "No, that's good."

"What was the question again? Say it again," Selina said with all frankness.

"What's a romantic way for a guy to let you know that he's interested in you?" I restated.

Faith looked at me like she finally saw the 3D picture in one of those murals you have to stare at for a while. She said, "Oh, that he's interested. The initial interest. To initially show that he's interested?"

"Yeah, the initiation," I kidded.

Selina started in as she asserted, "Well, I think the whole,

'Hey, I like you.' or 'Hey, my friend over there wants to know if . . .' That's so . . ."

"Lame," Faith summed up.

I couldn't believe it. More of the woman to woman telepathy.

"Don't do it. Ok? Do not do it," established Selina. "I think, if anything, if a guy's interested in you he'll become your friend first. He'll get to know you on a friendship level. Not trying to push you. Not trying to push the issue of, 'Hey, what's up with me and you?' Then through the friendship he'll find out, 'Like, is she even interested in me or not?' Or he'll find out through that if she is interested in someone else. So I think becoming friends with a girl beforehand to be romantic with her would be the best way to go. Because friendship is a way to get to know people."

Faith added, "Don't overdo it."

"Yeah," Selina corroborated.

"Don't rush," Faith voiced.

Selina's whole friendship remark kind of withered my hope. I mean, I was having a hard enough time finding a girl that I thought was right for me. Now, I was told that the best way to approach her when I finally did find her was as a friend. Then I would have to play the buddy role and go through the whole dreaded process of trying to find out who she had the hots for like I did in junior high. I needed more so I pressed on with the same line of questioning.

"So," I continued, "you said that becoming a friend first is the best thing. Are you saying that it's a good thing to go after friendship when you know you're already interested?"

"In that sense," Selina said after she had thought about my

question, "I think it would all depend on the girl. Say a guy liked Faith and he was very interested in her, but I knew she wasn't interested in him. If he comes up to me and says, 'Hey Selina, I'm interested in Faith and blah, blah, blah,' I'm gonna tell him, 'Don't pursue it, because I know she's not interested in you.' So it all depends on the girl, I think."

Wow, Selina is one tough little chick. Remind me not to get interested in her friends unless I've got a bandage for my wee heart. Seriously, though, just like in Proverbs where it says a frank reply is a blessing, I suppose that is what I would most like to hear if it were true. Yeah, it would hurt a little at the time, but it would save me from a lot more heartache later.

"Can you repeat the question?" Faith asked.

I told Faith, "I was just thinking; Selina was telling me how a good way to do it (*let a girl know you're interested in her*) is to pursue friendship before going after anything like that (*intimate relationship*). I was just asking her if that was a good idea even if you're initially interested in something more than friendship. To try to start the friendship."

"Oh, ok," Faith said. "Then again, I've heard stories of where the guy's completely interested and the girl wasn't. Over time, she would pray about it and she would actually have a list of people she would pray for. When she got to his name on the list, the Lord dropped something in her heart about him and she was like, 'Ok, Lord.'' Before that he would pursue her and pursue her—actually it's our pastor—and she did not like him. She was not interested at all. She would be like; 'Please let him leave me alone.' And now, look at them today: Married for what? 19 years?"

"Yeah," Selina agreed.

"So I mean . . . I don't know," Faith concluded.

I sat there for a moment trying to make sense of the girls' answers. Coming up with nothing, I spoke into the tape recorder playfully, "Thanks! All of this story was for nothing guys."

Selina and Faith got a kick out of that comment as they both started laughing.

So I guess we are kind of left out in the cold in regards to a black and white answer as to how persistent we should be with a girl we like. It really depends on whether or not it is a girl God is directing us to or one that we just happen to find extremely attractive. If it is merely the latter, which there is no shortage of, then you really have to be careful. Don't overexert yourself towards something God didn't direct you to. On the other hand, when God has guided you to a certain someone, then by all means be persevering! Just like anything else in life, don't give up on what God has called you to do.

Remember when God led the Israelites through the wilderness to the Promised Land, the land flowing with 'milk and honey.' Well guys, our wilderness is our journey to get to the woman whom we are to marry. That lucky lady is our Promised Land. Don't forget that when the Israelites finally made it to where they could observe the Promised Land they realized that there were giants inhabiting it. God told them to go in and whip some butt (my translation). Sadly enough, all of the Israelites ended up wandering around in the wilderness until almost all of those Israelites who could've gone in and taken the land had died. This happened because they were too afraid to fight for what God had given them.

Don't be like those Israelites. If God is telling you that a certain girl is your Promised Land, go in and fight for her! Be persistent. Pray about her. And by all means, don't give up! The Bible tells us to pray without ceasing . . . to keep on praying . . . to keep on keepin' on (1 Thessalonians 5:17 with some added emphasis). Remember that although God is all-powerful, as my pastor has said, "He always partners with His people to do the miraculous."

This is what Nehemiah conceived when he encouraged the builders that were trying to rebuild the wall around Jerusalem in 440 BC. Nehemiah and his crew overlooked many threats from their enemies. In Nehemiah 4:11 it tells of the danger Nehemiah and the workers faced daily. In that verse Nehemiah said, "Meanwhile, our enemies were saying, 'Before they know what's happening, we will swoop down on them and kill them and end their work.'" Now, knowing that God is almighty, Nehemiah called together the leaders and people and said, "Don't be afraid of the enemy! Remember the Lord, who is great and glorious, and fight for your friends, your family, and your homes!"

Nehemiah knew that, although God was great and glorious and could handle the situation by Himself, He required his people to be ready to fight by His side.

I also wanted to state my thoughts on guy-girl friendships. I think a lot of girls kind of see us guys as piggish because many of us don't seem to be looking for friendship before the relationship. Girls seem to have the idea that we should desire to be wholly friends with them with no underlying motives. In my opinion that's not the way we were meant to handle the situation.

Men and women are sexual creatures that are made to be intimately attracted to one another. Why can men buddies stay up late playing video games then zonk out on the same bed (dirty socks to faces) without any sexual feelings? Imagine trying to do that with a girl, even an unattractive girl. You get uncomfortable at best. Lust galore, at worst.

The fact is that men and women, as we have shown, are very different and thus, do not serve the same roles to each other. No girl can ever take the place of your male friends and conversely, none of us can substitute for a woman's female companions. Just imagine for a second if you did have a best friend who was a girl (which rarely happens without one of the parties being attracted to the other) and you got married to a different woman. How pleased do you think your wife is going to be with you chatting on the phone with your other woman friend? Not very! That is why it's impossible for women to have friendships with men like they have with other women and vice versa. After you get married, no additional woman should contribute anything to you that your wife could herself furnish for you. (Notice, I didn't say your wife 'does' furnish for you. Sometimes, we will be tempted to let other women do things that our wives should be doing, but aren't. That problem is only magnified when we have other women as close friends.) So if you do carry over close, opposite-sex friendships into marriage, they will have to be faded out soon thereafter.

So, in retrospect, there is nothing wrong with opposite-sex friendships as long as they carry a different meaning. Unless the couple is planning on going further into a marriage-minded relationship, boy-girl friendships should remain casual. That saves a lot of trouble down the road. But that's just my opinion, so you can take it or leave it (Just don't leave it without tender love. My opinions are very fragile.)

Now, with this mindset on casually being friends, I must concede that us guys should try to start our romantic endeavors with a foundational friendship. I think that my problem was that I thought that I couldn't like the girl if I was trying to be her friend. But that's just stupid. The fact is that I will never really know if I do like a girl unless I first become her friend. Again, I don't have to dissolve my hope that it will turn out to be more than friendship in order to try to be her friend. My sister said it this way, "It's not like if you both know you like each other you'll just instantly start making out. You'll become friends *because* you like each other." Such a casual friendship should show me if I should break it off, no feelings hurt, or pursue her as a girlfriend.

My only problem arises when girls think poorly of us men because we don't want do be involved in a deep friendship with no thoughts of it going further. We were not made to have those kind of friendships. (This is of course, unless you are called not to get married such as Jesus and Paul. Then it's a whole other ballgame that I don't know how to play. But if that's the case then you must've just read this far 'cause I'm so funny. Cool!)

My next question was brought about by my overall laziness. My mom always told me to open the door for my sister and do other nice, gentlemanly things for her. But, because my sister was a rough-and-tumble little brat when we were little (maybe I gave her one too many kisses when she was a baby), I quickly got out of the habit of doing chivalry-like deeds for women. I got lazy. I am just now finding the 'knight-inside-me' again and wondered what these damsels thought about it.

"Next one. Is chivalry really dead? Like a guy opening doors? Offering you his jacket? Stuff like that. Is that still good, or no?" I asked.

"Ohhhh noooo," Selina swooned, like she had just met Prince Charming. "That is great. I love that stuff."

Faith then responded, "And you know, as much as you hear about it being dead, I know a lot of guys who do that. A lot of guys who, like, open the door and . . . open the door . . .," Faith said trying to think of some other noble deed. Faith and I had a good laugh at her double 'open the door' comment.

Selina jumped in, saying, "For example, my cousin, he always opens the door. He always is like, 'Are you cold?' He'll give you his jacket. If he takes a girl out to dinner, even if they're just friends, he pays for her food. 'No, let me pay, please let me pay.' And I'm, 'No you don't have to, you're my cousin, gosh.'" (*Man, I wish some of my scuz bag cousins would buy me food, I thought. Just kidding. I love you guys. But really, though, buy me something.*) "That's how he was raised. Girls love that stuff. A lot of us watch old black and white movies and we're like, 'Oh my God! That's so beautiful!' and we're all crying, because that's just how we are. That's our make up. I don't know. Guys kind of brush it off sometimes, and I'm like, 'If you would just give that extra effort.'"

Faith compiled the girls' main thoughts as she stated, "I think chivalry is dead to people who don't expect it. I know that I'm worth more than just a McDonald's burger. To me chivalry is not dead because I'm expecting it. But, to some girls, chivalry is dead because, hey, all a guy has to do is look at them, and they're going with ya. It all depends on how you value yourself. We value ourselves, so to us, chivalry is very much alive."

"Right . . . Yeah," remarked Selina.

Christian Babe Alert

I agreed with Selina. That was a powerful statement.

"So if you wanna pursue this you better bring me chivalry. You better read a book or something. Watch those old black and white movies," Faith mandated.

"Better read this book," I said to plug my own book in . . . uh . . . my own book.

At that point I remembered a funny little thing that happened to me and my cousin Jake a few nights before. I decided to tell the girls about my story since it fit in with what they were discussing. We stayed up real late, after a hard night of video games. We decided to watch some TV, so we began to flick through the channels. Usually when we watch TV that late we catch some late infomercial selling baseball cards or something. You know the kind that say; "You'll get 50 different cards including a Ruth and Mantle rookie valued at $50,000 all for just seven easy, stretch payments of $12.99!" They never add up to reality, and so we usually have a blast ripping on them with the help of some late-night giggles. We are always careful, though, considering how many porno-like commercials and shows air that late.

So, anyway, I just happened to click and land on an old movie. I told the girls that as soon as my cousin and I saw it we just slumped back and went 'ahhhhhhhh.' Movies like that are like a breath of fresh air in the midst of today's programs that are clogged with sick junk. The funny part (besides the fact that I told you how me and my cousin –who both happen to be super tough and straight as arrows by the way- watched part of a girly movie), was the fact that before I even started making the 'ahhhhhh' sound, both girls were murmuring it simultaneously. For a second there, I felt like I was one with the universe.

I knew that, for the most part, women and men are on totally different wavelengths when it comes to interpreting acts of romance. For example, my dad thought he did a really romantic thing for my mom one day, not too long ago. He went up to her place of work and brought with him a bag of ripe cherries. All of the girls that work with my mom were thrilled and launched into a frenzy of admiration for my dad. Surprisingly, my mom was not so won over by the gift. You see, my mom doesn't really care for cherries. My dad loves them, though!

That seems to be what us guys tend to do a lot. We do what we enjoy rather than considering what the women might delight in. I wanted to find out some of the things that girls found pleasure in that us guys were clueless about so I said, "Ok, give me some examples of romantic things that guys could do, but that rarely crosses their minds. Like, you never see guys doing it, but you would want them to."

Selina immediately declared, "I think picnics. I love picnics."

"Yeah, like whisk me away somewhere," Faith added. "I think what I want my husband to do, is, like, call me at work and say, 'Meet me at so and so, I already packed a lunch and I packed your shoes. We're gonna have a picnic.' And then we go hiking. Surprise me!"

"Oh yeah," Selina said with excitement.

At that point Faith told me that if her husband did stuff like that she would be like, "Meet me in the bedroom, now!" So, you see, if we are willing to do the things that girls love they will definitely be more likely to provide us with what we want most. (Ohhhh yeah!)

(Unfortunately, at this point in the interview, Norwood took his last breath and recorded no more. Tragically, I didn't even realize what had happened until the end of the session. The following journalism will be a mixture of my phone calls with the ladies and the really neat things that stuck in my brain from the original, unrecorded, latter part of the interview.)

The next question on the agenda had to do with misuses of romance. Honestly, I'm somewhat of a 'romantic at heart.' The predicament that I find myself in is not having an object to aim my romance towards. I certainly use my romantic inclinations to do cool things for my family and whatnot, but I am forced to hold most of my ideas back until I find my babe.

To give you an example, consider what happened to me the night before I wrote this page in the book. I went out to get some grub at Friendly's with my friend Gary. Now, the Friendly's where I live serves some of the most mouth-watering burgers a man can handle, but that's not the reason I went there. I was feeling kind of lonely, with no particular direction from God yet (when it came to my babe-to-be). And there just so happens to be this really cute, dark-haired waitress at Friendly's. She's actually a little out of my league, but I'm expecting God to surpass my expectations, so I thought, 'Why not?' I wasn't sure how old she was or even if she was a Christian, but there was only one way to find out. I had gotten the chance to talk to her before, but I had never tried to go for the gusto.

I kind of like the 'finding-a-babe-at-the-restaurant' scenario. It's probably because of this guy I know named Jason. Jason and I were youth leaders together and Jason happened to have this very beautiful wife named Tanya. Years ago, when Tanya had just recently come over from Russia, Jason met her waitressing in some restaurant. (I can't seem to remember where. I mean c'mon, I can't recall all of the details.) She wasn't even a Christian at that time. Somehow, by some amazing miracle of God, Jason played the smooth card on Tanya and they started dating. Today they're married and are both strong Christians.

I'm not suggesting you go after non-Christian girls, I just wanted to submit the fact that, with God, all things are possible (Matthew 19:26). So I was at Friendly's waiting to be seated and hopefully show Gary this little babe when I realized that our waitress was going to be another girl altogether. I had seen this other girl that was now our waitress a few times before. (Yeah, so I eat out a lot!) The girl that was our waitress was really nice, but definitely not what I was looking for. Then, unexpectedly, the cutie that I had made the trip for popped her head out of the kitchen and made a mad grunt accompanied by an adorable pouty face because she didn't get to be our waitress. I filled myself up with all the boldness that I could muster, as I said, "Awwww, that's my girl. She always knows what I want." She then switched with the girl we currently had as our waitress (Which, I'm guessing is a no-no in waiter/waitress' etiquette) so she could serve us.

Let's just say that I've never been checked on that much at a restaurant before. My pop never ran out and neither did my anxiety. 'So why aren't I getting ready for a date with her?' you might ask. Well, when I was in the restaurant, getting all of that attention, I didn't feel God's nudge at all. I knew I couldn't just hunker down and pray about it right there in the middle of the restaurant. So I went to the bathroom and prayed. (A good thing to do when you're in a crowded situation but need to talk to God about something.) I stood in front of the grimy mirror and asked Jesus if this was the one for me. After a few seconds I knew she wasn't. (The only problem with my method was that I told Gary about me praying in the bathroom. Now every time I really have to use the facilities when we're eating somewhere, he thinks I'm praying about the waitress.)

Was I sad? Sure! Was I a little ticked at God for letting my hopes be crushed once again? You better believe it! To stop the funk that I was feeling from getting any crazier I just had to ask myself this question as if God Himself were asking me, "How great do you think I am?" That gave me time to realize that God was great enough to bring me another girl that was prettier than this last one. Because, let's face the facts, us guys all want a beautiful woman to like us.

All right, time to get back on track here. Last night I stayed up for some time thinking of all the romantic things I could have done for this girl, had God given me the 'green light'. Fortunately, I didn't let my romantic thoughts get out of control. When I asked Selina and Faith the next question it was with the foreknowledge that romance could get out of hand occasionally. I asked the girls, "Can being romantic go too far?"

Faith said, "Yes, it can. If the guy is using it to be manipulative, then it's gone too far. Or, if they are smothering the girl." Faith then pointed me towards an old episode of 'Frasier' to illustrate. She told me that, in one show, Frasier was jealous of his brother Niles' relationship and so he went overboard trying to better his own relationship by being excessively romantic. Frasier bought gifts galore for his girl, eventually suffocating her with his barrage of offerings.

I hadn't seen that Frasier episode, but since I was thinking of TV romance I was reminded of the 'King of Queens' program I had just watched. In it, Carrie, the exaggerated version of a whiny wife (she's sure hot though), told Doug, her husband without a clue, that she missed the old days when he used to be romantic. Their conversation resulted in Carrie pulling out an old box of priceless trinkets ranging from cards to a little stuffed frog. All of the items were things that Doug had given to Carrie in a meaningful way.

The next day Doug, who was lacking in the romance department, just started buying Carrie loads of lovey-dovey gizmos. Strangely enough, Carrie wasn't as gratified as Doug had expected.

Of course the show is funny because it's an embellishment of men's character flaws. So, just like Doug, we sometimes end up committing the same mistake Faith was talking about. We try to give our girls more of the gifts with less of the thought.

One of the principals of being romantic is to be thoughtful. Be creative! Try as hard as you can not to let embarrassment stand in the way. Some of the dorkiest things you could imagine doing will make the fondest memories for your woman. Don't buy just to buy, but always splurge on gifts that have mindful reasoning behind them. Instead of buying a dozen roses, pick some wild flowers, tie a string around them and author a note to go with them. The note could go as follows: first burn the edges with a lighter for effect, then write something like, 'God made your beauty like a wild river. It can't be contained by a single glance. So, I'm sorry if I stare.' Cool, huh?

If you make it a habit of thinking hard before you give, your gifts will never smother a girl.

Oddly enough when I called Selina to get her re-response to the question she said, "Yes, guys could smother you and, if it's to that point, then it's too far."

We got the point! Girls don't want to be smothered. Just keep in mind what I just talked about and also think back to what we talked about earlier regarding a girl that's not interested. In being thoughtful about your gift giving, you will quickly realize if a girl doesn't want gifts from you at all. In that case, save your money. It can be put to better use elsewhere.

Speaking of giving gifts . . . For my next question I asked Selina and Faith, "What is a great gift for a guy to get for you within the first two weeks of a relationship?"

Faith said, "Taking her out to eat. That's a good gift. Definitely not a Teddy Bear." Faith wasn't lying. She knew how to eat. The question was, *Where the heck did she put it all?*

As for the Teddy Bear, that was a whole other issue in and of itself. During the original interview, Selina had brought up her inner rage that she held towards stuffed animals. It seemed as though Selina, and even Faith, had been over-allocated with cuddly collectibles. I knew that the supply had far exceeded their demand as Faith hooted, "Tell me! Where am I gonna put it?" Not that all things stuffed are evil, but to these girls they were a 'no-win situation.' That's why you have to be creative, gentlemen. Because although girls exhibit many comparable traits, they are still unique enough to warrant individualized consideration.

Selina offered her advice on a good, early-on gift as she stated, "A single rose." That seemed to be her flower of choice.

Ok, now I was getting to the goods. The most thrilling and awaited part at the end of so many movies: The first kiss! For many of us guys we can't wait to go lip to beautiful lip with the girl of our dreams. Unfortunately, many Christian girls in this day and age are unsure as to whether or not they want to date, let alone kiss. Still I had to know. "When is a good time for a first kiss," I pried.

"After three or four months. If it is any sooner, it seems kind of rushed," Selina told me. I had to respect Selina's opinion, yet, on the inside, I was hoping it would happen a lot sooner for me.

Faith joked around with me as she said, "If you're not sure, you can do the lean in test." She then got more serious as she stated, "Kissing is kind of extreme when you first start dating. Especially if you haven't held hands for a while and watched some movies. So if you haven't done the simple things together, don't move on to kissing. That is a higher level of intimacy."

Both girls seemed to hint at the point that kissing is not to be taken lightly. Speaking of which, I still remember my first kiss on the lips. I was in third grade at a school in Pennsylvania. There was nothing around but acres of emerald meadows. My girlfriend was Patsy. She was gorgeous. As gorgeous as a tiny, eight-year-old girl could get. She was the envy of all of my buddies.

At recess time, while a horde of elementary kids darted around on the green grass, Patsy and I would walk around together holding hands. I even remember the way we held hands. No interlocking fingers, just her hand lightly cupped in mine. It was all so romantic. Actually I didn't even know what romance was back then, but I sure was becoming interested in girls.

Most every recess Patsy would give me a peck on the cheek. It was like a crown to my royal attire. My majestic robes were put on every time I got to call her my girlfriend. I was the king of the playground, or so I felt.

One very special day as I, the king, was about to get my kiss on the cheek, Patsy told me to look at her. Suddenly, without warning, our lips met. My eyes were wide open and it took a couple of seconds after the smooch had ended to really understand what had happened. I had kissed a girl on the lips! And not just any girl, but Patsy, the hottest babe I knew!

Yes, I'm sure Patsy and me were the talk of that little school community for some time. From then on we were kissing maniacs. Nothing nasty. Just little kid love. The funny thing was that, even though I didn't know what I was doing, I knew it was something special. It had to be pretty special for me to remember it to this day. I think the reason that my kiss with Patsy is forever engrained in my brain, is not only because it was my first, but also because it was pure.

By sixth or seventh grade you were pretty much expected to kiss your girlfriend within a fairly short time period. That expectation always made it awkward. You never really waited for the right moment, but rather did it almost out of duty. It was your job to kiss her within the first week. How else was she to know she was your girlfriend? That made all of those junior high kisses cheap and forgettable.

These girls I had been interviewing made me think about my most special kiss. I'm sure a lot of you guys have had a similar experience. The really cool thing is that we can have an even more memorable kiss if we are patient. Faith and Selina implied that we should not rush our inaugural kiss. I know that God has a unique moment set apart for something as modest as a first kiss. So just try to be like your younger self and wait until the time takes you by surprise.

For my next question I was sticking with the kissing phenomenon. This was a question more geared towards later in the relationship when kissing might be more common place. Heck, this information would even be helpful after marriage. I asked, "Where should a guy put his hands when he kisses you?"

Now, as you know, much of this part of the interview was recovered over the phone with the ladies. As for this question, however, I remembered some hilarious outtakes from the original conversation.

Immediately Faith went into a big spiel about how guys shouldn't mess with her hair. "Don't touch my hair!" she protested as she combed her hair behind her ears with her fingers. "I can do that myself," she said mockingly.

Faith and Selina then began to do fake kissing poses with each other which was making me laugh and get embarrassed all at the same time. After some kissing choreography, the girls had decided upon the best position for a guy to take. They both agreed that it is best when a man wraps his arms around a girl's back when he kisses her. Just so you could get a better idea of what the girls were talking about I've portrayed Selina and Faith's final product in the drawing on the following page.

For my next question, I inquired, "How should a guy initiate the patented arm around the shoulder, or holding your hand?"

"To me it is not comfortable holding hands," Selina said as she raved about the sweatiness of guys' palms. "The arm around the shoulder thing has to be as natural as possible. If he is too hesitant, it doesn't seem comfortable."

"Well, don't do the yawn because it doesn't work," Faith admitted.

I hope that everybody reading this book knows not to try the 'Zack Morris' yawn technique. The trick to establishing a cozy arm around the shoulder or an intimate holding of hands, as I learned from the girls, is to be confident.

Joyce Meyer explained something that had a very unanticipated connection to what we are talking about now. In one of her recent books 'Approval Addiction,' She took an in-depth look at the verse Proverbs 23:7. The verse reads, "For as he thinketh in his heart, so is he." Mrs. Meyer went on to show that people are usually perceived as they believe themselves to be. No, it was not some kind of over-spiritual hocus-pocus. It's not like she was saying you can just believe that you are six-foot-three and rich and you'll wake up the next morning to a butler saying, 'Breakfast is ready, sir.' Then you realize you can't leave the room because your 32-inch jeans now resemble mid-shin highwaters. She was just showing that if we believe people don't like us, we'll usually act in such a way as to alienate those very people. I've met a few people who didn't like themselves very much and it was equally hard for me to like them very much.

The point? Ahhhh, yes. When you are trying your little stud moves, believe that your babe is waiting for you to do them. Don't think, 'Oh man, I hope I do this right. I'm always so clumsy,' or you'll probably end up fumbling it up just like you thought. When it comes time for the arm maneuver, slide your muscles around that girl's back and pull her snug. Don't be super gentle either. We are men and women like that. (Oh yeah, pat your greasy little hands dry before touching her hand. That one was for all of those Selinas out there.)

I had finally made it to my last question, and boy was I

feeling the burn from the workout of this interview. In my experience, I have known some Christian men that I've respected that fell either to one extreme or the other on this next question. I wanted to know how far these girls felt it was appropriate to go before marriage. Of course, I was thinking about physical displays of love. I've met devoted Christian men who earnestly believed making out before marriage was perfectly fine. Then again, one of the most devout Christian dudes I have ever known, named Luvirt, wouldn't kiss his girl until they finally got married. As for me, I suppose I'm somewhere in between. I don't think I could handle the 'second base' (or whatever base making out is) scenario without hurting my conscience (i.e. getting it on.) But I definitely want to kiss my girl before we get married.

So I guess I kind of knew that this department of 'how far to go' was to be handled on an individual basis. Still, I wanted to hear what Faith and Selina had to say, so I simply asked them. "Some Christians think that you shouldn't kiss before you get married. Others think that it's ok to make out before marriage. What are your girls' opinions on how far is ok, in God's sight, before marriage?" I asked.

"I think before marriage, maybe we kiss, but I don't want to make out," Faith answered. "Because that can be so hard to break out of. Maybe a tender kiss, but not a passionate session. Keep it light. When you're done kissing, if he is wearing her lipstick, then they probably went too far."

Selina made the reply, "Mine personally . . . I want to wait for everything until after marriage. Most Christians think that kissing is ok. It's ok to do that in moderation because too much at one time could lead to something else."

Oddly enough, from my conversations with the girls I came to find out that Faith had never kissed a guy before, yet Selina had. Go figure.

At least the ladies shared the common thought that kissing (Not face slurping, guys!) was a standard barrier before marriage. Ahhh, that beautiful autumn night, as the leaves are clicking across the path and I look into her eyes . . . Oh, sorry. Got caught up in the moment there.

All I could really say was, "WOW!" Talking to girls and writing about it was exhausting. Not because I didn't like doing it. It was more like that drowsy feeling you get after scarfing down a huge meal. Faith and Selina had certainly given me a lot to think about. Yet, as I made my way to my car the night of the original interview, I couldn't help but feel dispirited due to the fact that I had lost so much of what the girls had said. (Remember my recorder homicide?) So, I was ecstatic to say the least when I ultimately got to see that the final result had turned out so well.

If there was one thing I had learned about romance from Selina and Faith, it was to 'take it slow.' That certainly didn't mean sit still like I used to think I had to do. Say that someone told you to drive slowly because the weather was bad. That wouldn't persuade you to stay inside your house until the rain stopped falling; it would simply mean that you should drive to your destination with caution. That is my single biggest problem with looking for a girl. I either want to chill at home and have God bring her to me like a mail-order bride or I want to rush out and find the right girl right away.

Just like there are people who drive like maniacs in adverse conditions, there will be people who tell you to hurry up and find your babe. As if your wife-to-be will marry someone else if you don't hustle. Check out what the man of admirable wisdom, Solomon, said. In Proverbs 19:14, it reads, "Parents can provide their sons with an inheritance of houses and wealth, but only the Lord can give an understanding wife." Yes! I love it when the Bible tells me that only God can do it. That takes the pressure off of us. This doesn't mean that we don't have to work to get our reward, but it does declare that the final outcome is not from our own efforts. It shows that we work at getting a wife because we know God is going to give us one, not because we might miss out on her. Again, there is a distinct similarity to salvation here. We do live righteously for God because we are so appreciative that He has already guaranteed our salvation. We don't do these things so that we can be sure we won't miss out on salvation.

Those people that make you want to rush, kind of lead you to feel almost as if God is hands-off in the situation. It's a good thing that Proverbs didn't say, 'but only you can get an understanding wife.' We don't have the power to obtain the wife God desires for us. We only have the capability of preparing ourselves for her and following God's directions to her. Trust me when I say that sometimes it feels like there are no solid directions. The reassuring thing is that God is very much watching over you, even though it may seem like you're all by yourself at times.

There is this verse in Isaiah that most of you guys have probably come across in one way or another. Isaiah 40:31 says, "But they that wait upon the Lord shall renew their strength; they shall mount up with wings as eagles; they shall run, and not be weary; and they shall walk, and not faint" (KJV). The other day, my pastor was preaching about this verse and his sermon paralleled my prolonged search for a woman. My pastor revealed the fact that 'waiting' didn't imply just sitting on the couch with a bag of chips. 'Waiting,' as the Bible intended it, did not at all mean inactivity, but rather an earnest expectation that leads you to be active.

A quick example has to do with my best friend, Jake. Whenever he tells me he's coming over to play video games it could either mean he'll be knocking at my door in three and a half seconds or I'll be waiting for him for an hour. It's kind of like a little game he likes to play on his poor, older cousin. While I am waiting for Jake, I never just flop out on the couch and moan, "Ohhhhh . . . When will he ever get here!" (Ok, I occasionally do that.) But I usually clean a little or set up the systems, sporadically peering out the window to see if he's here yet.

I'm not quite as efficient while waiting for my babe. I do whine to God a lot, saying, "Ohhhh . . . When will I meet her, Jesus?!" But I have learned to wait a lot better than I used to. I keep up with my Bible reading and relationship with God. That's comparable to my cleaning while waiting for my cuz. I also am constantly bettering my characteristics that I know will help me with the ladies, similar to how I prepare the game systems to be played when Jake arrives. Furthermore, I am on the lookout for a girl. I don't just pass them all by without frequently forcing myself to start a conversation and checking for sparks. And yes, that would be like me being watchful for Jake's car to coast into the driveway. The key is that I believe that Jake is coming over when he told me he would be. I think it is truly important to, no matter how long we end up waiting, believe and trust that God will come through for us as well.

I'm not smart enough to say how God will lead you to be active during your waiting period. You may feel the need to date some women. You just might be so consumed with your work for God that you hardly notice your future wife googling over you. I believe the waiting process is catered by God to be just what you need and thus is different for everyone.

Don't feel horrible if you are doing what you feel God wants you to, but you can't get your mind off that impending day when you will find a babe. Others might tell you, as they have me, "You'll find her when you're least thinking about her." That just makes you think about her more while you're trying not to think about her. It's true that many good men have found their wives when they were least engrossed with anticipation for them. But it is equally true that a myriad of Christian men have found their girls while they were eagerly searching for them. Just think about Christmas. Some people forget that they have a present under the tree and thus it is a great excitement to them when they open it and are super surprised. Then there are people who know what they are getting and get happy feelings just looking under the tree at that beautiful present. They wait, with enthusiastic anticipation until they finally get their hands on their gift early on Christmas morning. Neither person is wrong.

I think that people tell you that you will only find her when you aren't pondering the situation because it sometimes seems that way. This is the best and most simplistic correlation I can think of to show why. Consider any time when you are driving somewhere and you are in a huge hurry. Late to work? Trying to make it to church on time? Whatever. Then, as you are speeding down the road you see that picturesque green light flip to yellow. As the yellow light smirks at you, taunting you to speed up even faster in order to blow through it before the red demands that you stop, you slow down, all ticked off, knowing you probably couldn't make it.

Now, you know you have to wait for this red light just like we might know we have to wait for God to give us a girl. This is where I learned something amazing. If you just sit there and stare at the red light waiting for it to turn green it will seem like it is the longest freaking red light in the history of humanity. But, if you grab your smartphone out of your console and start browsing the web, that light will turn almost instantly. Of course, that good old, metal light box didn't change any faster because you were scanning your favorite website, but your perception made you think it did because your focus wasn't hovering on the traffic light.

It's kind of the same thing while waiting for your beauty. It might seem like it takes forever if you are constantly preoccupied with thoughts of her. If you can set your focal point on something else, however, it may seem like God moves a lot faster. I believe that God has a perfect time for you to meet that girl, though, whether or not you think about her. Just like the light, God will let you "go" at His prescribed time no matter if you are waiting like a crazed Christmas morning kid, or if you were somehow able to occupy your time with other matters, or even if you bobble back and forth. Just don't run the red light.

I'm just taking a wild and crazy guess when I say that you are most likely the kind of person that is in pursuit of your woman even though you may be undergoing God's waiting period right now. Even though that sounds paradoxical, it really isn't all that uncommon. I'll use one of the examples my pastor utilized. Picture yourself going to the doctor's office. You got yourself a 10:30 appointment to get that foot fungus taken care of. Good job, you healthy stud, you. Now, do you really think that when you waltz into that drab waiting room at 10:28, you'll immediately be whisked away into a check-up room? Of course, we all know that once we get to the waiting room we do exactly what the name implies . . . we wait.

That doesn't mean that we should stay clear of the doctor. (You have that nasty fungus, after all.) Nor should we just slink back in the germ-filled seat in the waiting room with our fingers up our noses, getting madder for every second we have to linger. Instead we pick up a magazine and read, or we cycle through the questions we want to ask the doctor. Just because we have to wait doesn't mean we aren't planning on meeting the doctor. We have an appointment after all. And, likewise, each and every one of us has an appointment with a beautiful woman as long as we seek God's will. The Bible says it this way, "Seek His will in all you do, and He will direct your paths." That verse is found at Proverbs 3:5.

All right, now that I knew I was actively waiting for the opportunity to be romantic and exercise some of the tactics I had learned from these two beauties, I had to get some information on another topic. In case my active waiting lead me to the dating scene soon (fingers crossed), I wanted to get the inside scoop on how to conduct myself in a dating situation, as well as where to go and a number of other things. So I wrote myself a note to finish up the book with a dating and conversation interview. But first, I had to check in with my gorgeous and bratty little sister for interview number three.

INTERVIEW TROIS (3)

SNOT-NOSED SISTER INTO INSIGHTFUL SIBLING

Babe Talk

'All heart,' or 'back off, if you're smart.'
When I checked with 20 beauties to see whether they preferred
a sweetheart or a bad boy:
30% desired a bad boy,
45% wanted a sweetheart,
and 25% said they craved a little of both.
"I want a guy with a sensitive side, but I don't want some wussy-boy who's more emotional than me." —Maria

SNOT-NOSED SISTER INTO INSIGHTFUL SIBLING

When I was younger I used to go into overdrive in loving my baby sister, Maria. I used to sneak a kiss on her pudgy little cheeks every chance I got. She would always scrunch up her face like she had just sucked a lemon and yell to my mom to tell me to stop, but I couldn't help myself.

One fond memory I have of her puts me back in the kitchen at about age 5. My sister was about two and a half. At that age she was adorable, but her diet was extremely odd. The girl would eat most condiments as if they were the main course. A tiny handful of mayonnaise straight from the jar? You better believe it. How about a chunk of butter, forget the bread? Oh yeah. One thing she loved that I couldn't fault her for was cake frosting. This particular day my mom, who tried to limit my sister's weird dietary obsessions, walked into the kitchen as the refrigerator door closed. My mom asked Maria what she was doing. Maria said, "Nuffing," in a tiny, nervous voice. My mom then asked her if she had eaten anything. Maria told her no, as her chubby face, covered in green, Betty Crocker frosting, testified against her.

Then we got older. We grew up to be teenagers and I began

to see my sister as a spoiled brat. Even after I became a Christian, I thought things would never change. I saw my sister as doomed to remain in the realm of brattiness for the rest of her days. Fortunately, she has taken great strides towards mature womanhood. Nowadays, although a tiny bit of brat still stays with her, there is way more of that little girl I used to love so much.

My sister has been married for a little over a year now. (Yes, my younger sister beat me to wedlock and, yes, I am very salty about it.) And, even though I initially didn't want to interview any wedded women, I just had to scrutinize my sister's womanly wisdom. You see, the cool thing about talking with my sister is that she is brutally honest with me. In the other interviews my boyish charm hypnotized the girls into answering with more fanciful replies. Just kidding. But there was definitely an openness that I received from my sister that I just couldn't get from a friendly acquaintance.

This inescapable frankness even helped me to pinpoint the accuracy of my writings. Throughout the process of writing this book, I would let my sister read over my manuscripts. Then I would ask for her input. It seemed as though she almost always agreed with what these girls were telling me. Since she certainly isn't one to dance around the issue of telling me when she doesn't like something I've done, every one of her compliments was quite reassuring.

My sister has grown up to be a stunning young woman, both in beauty and godliness. Yeah, I know, you're probably saying, 'Dang, this guy only interviews pretty girls.' Hey, I can't help it. God gave me a bunch of babes to interview. It's not like I'm going to argue with Him about that. (A lot of guys would certainly consider my sister to be a babe, so that's why I threw her in there.) Anyway, I used this time with my sister to gather some info that could definitely be useful to us guys that are bitin' at the bit to get a girl to marry.

So, one evening, I invited my 23-year-old kid sister over to my house. I hopped into the big, blue cushions of my living room couch as she took a seat on the floor, with her back reclining on the puffy love seat. I opened up my small leather book that contained my questions and set Norwood (resurrected from the dead) to record as I once again began my quest for knowledge.

To start off I want to say that my sister's choice for a husband had eluded my original expectations for her. Don't get me wrong. After seeing them together I now realize that Tom, her husband, was hand-selected for her by God. Tom has the perfect personality to compliment my sister. (By that I mean Tom has tons of patience to deal with her. Just kidding, Bratty Brookeless. Oops. Did I accidentally type the nickname I gave my sister, Maria Brooke Emery, when she was younger?) The thing was that when Maria was maturing into a dating diva I always pictured her acquiring more of a model-esque man.

I decided I'd ask my sister how Tom pulled her in from the get-go. I began the interview as I asked, "What made you immediately attracted to Tom?"

"His confidence . . . 'Cause I've told you this story a million times," my sister said as if she were distressed to have to tell me again.

Yes, I knew how the story went. But I got her to retell the whole tale as I skillfully played it off by remarking, "Tell me again because my brain's rusty."

Christian Babe Alert

"I was talking to somebody that I didn't know at college before class," my sister said. "And Tom came up and just started talking to us and I didn't even see him because I was sitting on the floor and they were both standing up."

Why my sister was sitting on the floor at college, I will never know.

My sister continued, "And then he just started talking to us and I was like, 'Oh, he must know this kid.' He didn't even know either one of us. He just started talking in our conversation."

"What the heck?" I replied. "So it wasn't like fake confidence?"

"No, he just talks to whoever he wants to talk to," my sister told me.

Well, that sounded simple. I mean everybody talks to who they want to, right?

Well, if you're anything like me then the answer is, 'Heck no!' There are so many times I want to talk to a girl but the courage meter just won't fill up. This almost happened the night I interviewed Selina. When I saw her that night at church, it was ridiculously hard to ask her if she was ready for the interview. She was talking to a group of her friends and it was almost as if there was this inner battle going on inside of my mind as to whether or not I should even approach her.

The good guys in my head were engaged in intense combat, telling me that I should just go over to her and ask her if she was ready. The baddies in my brain were fighting to the death to gain ground on the hill of self-esteem. They were struggling to persuade me that I would look like a fool walking over to Selina and her friends all by my lonesome. Even though the good won out that night, it would have been tremendously easier if only I could have remembered my own sister's account.

When Tom approached Maria she was already talking to someone else. Yet, he persisted to interject himself into the discussion. Tom understood an awesome little fact that seems to live in the back of most of our minds already, but rarely pushes us to act. Tom knew that people wanted to talk to him.

Sounds a little conceited, doesn't it? Well, it's not. Conceited would be not caring if people want to talk to you. Most of the time people want to be talked to. Girls are no different. My biggest problem is that although I know most any given girl would appreciate some attention from me, I often feel quite differently.

First of all, when I say 'most girls would value me talking to them,' I'm not saying that I'm Gaston from Beauty and the Beast. You know, the guy that made little hearts bubble out of any girls he passed. I'm merely saying that it is a fact that everybody enjoys stimulating conversation.

Secondly, we often know something is true although we feel otherwise. Take knowing that God is near you, for example. The Bible clearly states, on multiple occasions, that God will always be close to us (Joshua 1:9 and Matthew 28: 20 to name a couple places). Still, there will be plenty of times when we feel like we are the farthest thing from God, although we know it's not true.

The thing that I have learned is to always follow what you know even when it contradicts what you feel. Not that God won't use feelings to assure you that what you are doing is right, sometimes. It's just that God won't let your feelings change His truth. So, our feelings can't change the truth, but the truth can alter the way we feel. For instance, just because you feel dismal inside won't change the fact that it is a sunny, gorgeous day outside. On the other hand, the simple reality of beautiful weather could in fact uplift your attitude.

So this all adds up to the fact that we have to put our feelings in check. You may feel like talking to a girl would make you look like a total stalker. Don't accept it! Simply accept the truth that the girl would actually enjoy talking to you over the lie your emotions are telling you.

So what makes a lot of us guys so apt to shy away from talking to girls? It pretty much boils down to fear. I'm not talking about the 'killer clown outside my shower curtain' kind of fear. I'm thinking more along the lines of fear of rejection, fear of failure, and fear of the unfamiliar. And don't think for a second that this is restricted to guy-girl relationships. This is a people problem.

I just recently started substitute teaching at my local high school. I have noticed this problem exists on a pretty basic, but wide-scale, level there. Being a substitute I am all over the building and I see a lot of teachers, but I haven't gotten a chance to know many of them yet. The first thing that I noticed while subbing is the fact that some teachers won't even say 'Hi' to me as I pass by and many of them wouldn't even think of really talking to me. At first I was kind of mad, thinking they were a bunch of sub-haters. Then I realized that they, just like me, were scared to reach out to unknown faces. They were probably nervous about how I would react to them, even though I really needed some attention. Thankfully, God provided me with some buddies already, but I certainly don't want to follow the current trend of fearfully avoiding interactions. I mean, doesn't it just feel good to have a stranger pass you and nod to you as he says, "Hey, how ya' doin'?" knowing full well that he's just being friendly?

So what do we do? Just the other day I actually learned something that might help. We need to be courageous. Yeah, I know, that sounds like some medieval mumbo-jumbo. The thing is that a lot of us, myself included, have seen being courageous as something it's not. We envision armored knights galloping on their noble steeds. We picture Joshua sprinting down a grassy slope, sword drawn, as he engages in a battle torn from the 'Lord of the Rings' movies. We imagine young David as he stood with his sling dangling at his side after he had slain the magnificent Goliath. We see courage in all of this, but unfortunately, we don't perceive ourselves to be anything like that. We see courage as something you either have or you don't. And if you are sometimes scared, you most likely don't.

At least that was my view until I did an odd thing. I have this little key chain that has Joshua 1:9 engraved on it. In Joshua 1:9, the Lord commands Joshua to be "strong and courageous." God had told Joshua this because he was the one that was going to enter the Promised Land and thus had the fun job of defeating the hordes of wicked locals that inhabited it. Joshua's assignment from God was to lead the Israelites to conquer this unknown land while sticking to every letter of God's law. Talk about needing courage!

Then, just the other day I was sitting in the teacher's lounge at the school where I was subbing. I was reading in 1 Chronicles 28:20 and noticed that David tells his son, Solomon, the very same thing. "Be strong and courageous . . . Don't be afraid or discouraged," he said. I guess that the saying is intended to be passed on from generation to generation. So, in order to get a better understanding of what was being said, I popped open my leather bag and pulled out my fat, red dictionary. I keep a dictionary in there so I can look smart when the kids ask me how to spell something. I flipped through the old yellow pages until I saw the word 'courage' typed in a bold font. The definition read, '\ker-ij\ n : ability to conquer fear and despair.'

Let me take a second to relate to you what that meant to me. First, it told me that we don't just have all courage or no courage. Courage is an ability. And just like all other godly abilities, it can be built up even if you feel as though you're starting off with very little. Here's a quick example: Last year I was doing my student teaching in an urban school in Cleveland, Ohio. I'm a white dude, but the school had a good mix of black kids, white kids, and Hispanic kids. I know that's not very politically correct, but I don't need to be in order to let the kids know I love them all the same. Now, it just so happened that my mentor teacher (the math teacher whom I student taught under) was the eighth grade basketball coach for the girls' team. So, when it came time for the faculty basketball game, where the teachers square off against the eighth grade boys' team, my mentor and I were asked to play.

Now let's get this straight: I'm pretty athletic, but I was the typical stereotype of a white basketball player. I had very little ability when it came to hoopin' it up. Luckily, my cousin Jake breaks the mold of the goofy white b-ball player. He's really good. So I played with him for a couple months before the game.

Day after day I would face off against him or practice at the YMCA. By the time game day came, I had improved quite a bit. Don't get me wrong. When I got out on that scuffed-up, parquet floor I was pretty nervous at first and I didn't end up looking like the star. But, more importantly, I did end up fitting in. Hey, I even swooshed the only shot I took. My ability went from somewhere near zero to a respectable medium in a short time because I was focused on making it better. Imagine if I had kept playing. I would probably be in the NBA right now instead of writing this book. You guys really lucked out.

The good thing is that once you start to amplify your ability to be courageous you will never stop and you'll only get better!

Finally, these verses told me that you shouldn't feel horrible if you get scared sometimes. Remember courage is not the absence of fear, but the ability to conquer it. Joshua could not have conquered the Hittites, the Amorites, the Canaanites, etc., had he not fought them in many different battles. Similarly, you cannot conquer fear without fear being present to fight. Fear might overtake you a lot at first, but, remember, it's who wins the war, not the individual battles, that counts. And you, my friend, will win the war!

(Oh yeah, about that despair part. Despair is nothing more than discouragement. When you feel discouraged in your quest for a woman, fight it! And you will be strong and courageous!)

At this point in the interview with my sister I wanted to ask her about fake confidence. I wanted to know how girls can tell the difference between a guy that is confident enough to talk to a girl when he doesn't even know her and the kind of cocky guy that can't help but show himself off to every girl he sees. I asked, "How can you tell the difference between fake confidence and real confidence. Like guys that are conceited, kind of?"

"Because you can just tell they're fake. You can tell when people try too hard. Or when they're just being themselves and they just think what you are talking about is interesting and they want to talk about it too. Like Bo Bice. He's fake," Maria said, taking a stab at my pick for American Idol, 2005.

I had a few giggles at my sister's wit as I said a few choice words under my breath.

I continued the questioning as I said, "Tell me a few romantic things that Tom has said to you."

"I'm trying to think, because I know there are a few things he's said," my sister began as she tried to remember.

"I hope so! You married him!" I interrupted with zeal.

"He tells me I'm the most beautiful person all the time," my sister stated.

"Is that a big thing to a girl?" I pried, although I already knew the answer.

My sister looked at me in awe as she said, "Yeahhhh," in a Valley Girl tone. "Cause they want to be the prettiest to you," she continued.

My next question to my sister stemmed from the dusty, old saying, 'The grass is always greener on the other side.' I know it sounds like something your grandmother would say as she rocked you to sleep in your crocheted blankie, but it's actually a very powerful statement. The fact is that we all know of things that we look at and say, 'Man, if I only had that, my life would be a lot better.' And that's a good thing. It's good to hope for things we don't yet have. But sometimes we get so caught up in gawking at those things, we lose sight of what we do have right now.

I know, in my life, for example, I sometimes get so enveloped in my hopes of a girl that I don't appreciate my single life as much as I should. I know there will be things that I will miss as a married man, like playing video games through all hours of the night. I wondered if my sister could give me any details about what she misses the most about her single life. Then I could maybe cherish what I have a wee bit more while I still had time.

"What are some things you miss about being single that you can't do anymore," I questioned.

My sister thought for a second and then replied, "Have guy friends."

"Why do you miss that?" I asked.

"Because all of my friends used to be guys and I just kind of had to stop talking to them. And it's just weird to have guy friends after you get married," my sister expressed.

Now that I think about it, my sister was always freakishly strong when she was younger and that probably made it easy for her to fit in with the dudes. She could outrun me for the majority of my young life.

"Anything else?" I prodded.

"I miss that first time you like someone. Going out on dates and stuff. Because after you get married the excitement kind of goes away and you have to work hard at having fun," my sister told me.

Even though I already knew about that dismal fact it still was depressing to hear it. It is the reality of humanity that we all get bored with what we've got. It kind of reminds me of the Second Law of Thermodynamics. You start with something magnificent, but eventually through the rigors of time it breaks down into something mundane. For those of you not wanting to break out your ninth grade science book, the Second Law of Thermodynamics is a universal law that asserts that if any system is left to itself it will inevitably move from a state of order to disorder.

It is a sad but true fact about the world we are living in that has been empowered by the very curse of God. In Genesis 3:17 God said to Adam, "Because you listened to your wife and ate the fruit I told you not to eat, I have placed a curse on the ground. All your life you will struggle to scratch a living from it. It will grow thorns and thistles for you, though you will eat of its grains. All your life you will sweat to produce food, until your dying day. Then you will return to the ground from which you came. For you were made from the dust, and to the dust you will return." God told Adam that his wonderfully complex body would someday become nothing more than the dirt under his toes.

It is the same with the wondrous relationship that awaits us in marriage. The flames of our youthful passion will sooner or later die out like a day-old campfire. All that will be left are the blackened, smoldering remains of the coals that once held that molten orange glow.

I would let you have a second to cry about the dreary picture I just painted regarding your future, but that's not where the story ends.

To illustrate I have to go back a few years to when I first got my driver's license. Or, better yet, when my cousin, Jake, first got his. Just like any normal, soon-to-be driver, Jake was ecstatic. He was revved up with anticipation as he awaited the day he could drive himself around. Up until that point, I had been the designated chauffeur. Prior to getting his license Jake would often crack a huge smile as he told me, "Dan, when I get my license I will drive us everywhere! I will always drive for all of the times that you drove."

"Jake," I would say, "trust me when I tell you that you'll be sick of driving in six months."

Ok, so I was wrong. It only took about three months. I think getting a driver's license has a big correlation to getting a girl. Before you actually get either one, you are so excited about the way it will change your whole world for the better. And it does. Well, at least for a little while. Then you start to reminisce about the good ol' days when you actually had other people driving for you. Or the days when you could just go out with your buddies at anytime without worrying about your other half.

It seems like the Second Law of Thermodynamics has us pinned down. Whatever we find that is good in due time turns into a mess of regrets, or, at best, a ball of ho-humness. No matter how many times you try to convince yourself that you will never tire of your wife, you are only playing the naïve role of my younger cousin Jake. You can assure yourself that the sex will flow like wine, but sooner or later, your wife won't enjoy it as much as you do. She will suddenly come down with a case of the hanky-panky-induced headaches.

But wait. There is a God-given loophole!

When we look at the Second Law of Thermodynamics we notice that it specifically targets 'any system left to itself.' Just as if we were to continually toss logs on a campfire to keep it burning, we don't have to leave the system to itself. The thing is that to avoid imminent decay we can't leave things to themselves. We have to be involved.

This is why my sister was saying how she and her husband have to work hard to have fun. We will all have to work hard to maintain the fire that exists at the beginning of our marriage. It's kind of like a dirty room. I know all about this, because my room has been dirty since I was two. We all know that if we sleep in our room and do nothing to keep it clean, it will eventually get messy. At the very least it'll fall into the devious hands of dust mites. Then again, if we exert a little effort regularly we can keep our rooms fairly spotless. The same goes for our relationships. This is the sentiment the women of Jerusalem presented in chapter 2, verse 15 of the Song of Solomon. They told the young lovers, "Quick! Catch all the little foxes before they ruin the vineyard of your love, for the grapevines are all in blossom."

The problem arises when we neglect to clean for a while and the next thing we know our floor is covered by an ocean of dirty clothes and a smelly piece of food that we can't seem to locate. Then the problem has gotten so big that we don't know where to start, and, so, we don't. The growing filthiness overwhelms us and we just give up.

The same thing happens in a lot of marriages. Especially Hollywood marriages. Remember when Brad Pitt and Jennifer Aniston got together? When they got hitched, it seemed like the ideal marriage. Two picture perfect people with hearts of gold. They *had* to stay married forever. I mean, look at how flawlessly they fit together. Even Peanut Butter and Jelly couldn't be considered a better designed couple. But, like most glamorous movie-marriages, it fell apart. Why? Because marriages don't work depending on the outward appearance, but, rather, they rely on what each person is willing to do on the inside. If we think that our initial passion will carry us into 'til death do we part,' we've got another think comin'. That would be like thinking you could buy a brand new house, never clean it, and yet it would remain gorgeous looking.

One of the biggest ways to keep that fire going is to try hard not to forget what it was like before you found her. Now that's easy to say, but difficult to do. A good way that I have found to practice for this task is to try to be happy about driving.

I know, I know. You hate driving, right? I'm sure nobody ever wants to drive you around and let you just recline back in the passenger seat. And gas prices are so stinking expensive! Well, try to remember what it was like before you could drive. Remember when you were so anxious to get away by yourself, but you were forced to rely on other people to get almost anywhere? For me it brings back memories of my mom dropping me and my friends off at the mall. As I would get close to the mall's glass entrance, a good distance from our massive Econoline van, I would hear my mom's voice echoing across the parking lot. She would yell, 'I love you, Sweetie! I'll be back at nine.' Maybe my memories have grown a tad out of proportion, but they still warrant my thankful attitude when it comes to my privilege to drive.

Ok, it was on to my next question. As my sister gazed at me waiting for my next inquiry I spouted out, "What are like the major changes for a woman in married life? Like, when you go from single life to married life?"

After a long pause she responded. "Pretty much, you have to do everything for the man," she said as her voice trailed off into laughter.

"Wowwwww," I said in a sarcastic kind of tone.

"No," my sister interrupted. "They're like someone you have to take care of because they don't do stuff for themselves."

As I snickered to myself my sister voiced, "I'm serious. I literally—when he goes to work for eight hours—have to pack him a lunch and tell him to eat."

At least no girl will ever have to worry about reminding me to eat. Still, I knew what my sister was yapping about. Us guys definitely like to be pampered. I mean we can take a blow to the nose and not run home for help, but if we catch the slightest cold we need 100% womanly attention. If not from our wife, then from our mom.

Fortunately most of us Christian young guys are learning how to be independent when it comes to our careers. We know how to go to work every morning and put in a full day of dealing with every job-related stress imaginable. On the other hand, we aren't too accustomed to doing anything that mom used to or still does do for us. Washing clothes? Doesn't that machine do that? Preparing food? Yeah, it's just there. Hot and steaming when you're hungry, right?

I think a lot of fresh marriages start to spoil because guys tend to think that their job is over once they're done at the office, factory, school, or wherever they make the coinage. Try not to think that way. I'm not saying that you'll have to do your wife's job for her, but learn now to be willing to help her out when the time comes. The important thing is to shoot down this thought whenever it comes into your head: "Why do I have to help her with her job? What does she do to help me out with mine?" Those kinds of thoughts will only bring strife and anger. Try hard to think of the stuff she does do. How about shopping for and packing your lunch? Try to go to work one day and skip eating lunch. You'll quickly realize how important such a little effort really is. Then again, like the ladies from the first interview helped me realize, you and your woman might both be working long hours. In that case, work at home will definitely be split down the middle. So either way, it's good to start practicing and getting good at these everyday responsibilities now.

You might be thinking, "Yeah, no problemo. I'll help my wife out with the little stuff once I get one." Well, if you don't start working on it now you probably won't do it once the pressures and business of marriage roll around.

This reminds me of something my sister asked me to do a couple of days ago. She is building this little model of a library for her college project. She wanted me to make her a minute replica of Michelangelo's David statue that he sculpted back in 1501. She even had a corner of her library roped off with some bright red pipe cleaners just waiting for my work of art to arrive. (By the way, if I had known my work would have consisted of molding a naked David, I probably would've asked her to give me another piece of art to duplicate.) Anyway, it was Thursday when she first asked me and she needed it by Monday or something. (I wasn't really paying attention.) I had the strong inclination inside me to wait until Sunday to do my work on it. After fighting my love for procrastination I got to work on it Saturday morning instead.

Not that I couldn't finish it all on Sunday, but I knew it would be cutting it close. In order to secure a peaceful Sunday for myself I had to do work beforehand. That's kind of how it is with babes. Better start working now or it'll be really hard later.

I mean, isn't it so much better to be assured that you know how to do something before people actually depend on you to do it?

So I suggest you take it slow by doing some tasks that you normally wouldn't that will soon be a blessing to your destined babe. (Speaking of which, I'll be taking a quick break from typing to fold some towels.) One last thing though, before I go to the land of fabric softeners: You don't need to deprive your girl of her innate nature to nurture in order to help her out. Every opportunity that you have, enjoy her caring for you as only a woman can. But don't let her burn herself out. Be prepared to give her the help she will need.

My sister wasn't quite done with my question. (Remember, the question was, "What are the major changes for a woman in married life".) She kept her reply alive as she stated, "Making dinner is another one, too, because I never really cooked."

"You're a good cook now though, right?" I said to give a friendly word of encouragement.

"Yeah, I'm the best," my sister said a little too seriously.

"Ok, you went too far," I said.

I was just about to go onto the next question as I said, "Ok," when my sister interrupted.

"Wait," she blurted out. "I would have to say, like, um, communicating. That's a big deal and you think you don't do it enough."

Maybe that's why most girls never shut up. You *are* a guy reading this book, right?

I knew I sometimes got overloaded on how much some women in my life wanted to talk to me. (Don't get the wrong idea. They're related to me.) I asked, "So, what advice would you give to build that up before you get married?"

"You just have to whenever you get mad or any kind of feeling. You have to talk about stuff," my sister responded. "Because even if you feel like you don't need to talk, you do. And it's annoying."

There was a good point in what my sister had just said. Talking is annoying. Just kidding. But there is some truth there. If you've ever come home from an exhausting day of work and your (place any female relation here) wants to 'talk about it' before you get a chance to rest, then you can understand where I'm coming from. The fact of the matter is that when you get a woman there will be a 99.979% chance that she will want to talk about stuff more than you do. And, since communication is such a vital part of any relationship, it is good to force yourself to converse more now so you don't get ticked off at your wife later.

Once in a while just turn off the TV, turn to your (mom/sister/whomever) and ask her how her day was. In order to make yourself interested, ask questions and quiz yourself (in your head of course) on what she just said. After a few times doing that you might just start to care a little. Do this even when, like my sister said, "You feel like you don't need to talk". It'll pay some major dividends later in life.

After hearing my little sister's recommendation I said, "Good advice."

"Thanks, Daniel," my sister said with flair.

"You're welcome, Maria," I added as I moved on to my next question.

I really just wanted to see where God fit into my sister's marriage. I knew she was a strong, young Christian woman that didn't over-spiritualize stuff. By that, I mean I knew she wouldn't answer my next question with a bunch of churchy lingo in order to prove to me that she was a "bigger than life" Christian. Since I wanted real life, applicable answers, I asked my sister, "What role does God play in marriage, for you, so far?"

"A big one," my sister said in a dazed, hippie tone of voice. "Just, like, everything we do we try to do, like, according to what He wants. Whenever we just stop and pray about something or think about what we should be doing it always works out. And whenever we kind of forget about that, stuff just goes wrong."

"I like that," I said, happy to hear that my baby sister checks in with God. That's definitely some valuable advice. We, as men, need to learn how to consult God about stuff. One Sunday morning I remember hearing my pastor talk about how he had checked with some of the people around him about a decision he had to make before he asked the advice of God. He said that his mother-in-law later came up to him and told him that he needed to ask God before he got the counsel of men.

A lot of times it's just easier to ask people around us what they think rather than to ask God and have to wait for His answer. And there is nothing wrong with considering the opinions of wise people, but after hearing my pastor talk about his uncertainty I try to make sure I ask God first. Sometimes God wants me to heed the advice of other Christians and sometimes he just straight out answers me Himself, but He never neglects to guide me when I come to Him first.

My sister summed it up by stating, "Yeah, that's like true for anything though. But it's the same for marriage. God is like the same amount of importance."

How true. And that is why if we value God in our lives now, before we find a girl, He will continue to be important in our lives after we get married.

All right, I had just about had enough of my punk little sister so it was onward to my final question of the day. You hear so many women talking about how their couch potato of a husband is not the same strapping young lad they had married. I knew that was bound to happen to me, in some respects at least. When I get more comfortable with my hottie, in the future, I will most likely let my guard down a tad and some of my more irritating traits may come out to play. The thing that I wanted to capture from my sister was which of those things that guys tend to let out only 'after the ring is on the finger' (as Sylvia pointed out earlier) are really damaging to the relationship.

I stared at my sister, who was nestling into the front of the love seat, and said, "What is one thing guys relax on after you get more comfortable with them . . . married, whatever, that you wish they wouldn't?"

My sister didn't waste any time as she spurted out, "Like, their dressing. And the cleanliness and the smell. Pretty much everything they do to get the girl, they just stop."

I jotted down some final notes as I laughed out loud at my sister's list of what Tom doesn't do anymore. Well, that reply was pretty self-explanatory. Just like how we wouldn't want to come home and see our newly wed wives in saggy sweat pants with their hair tangled up in a greasy pony tail, your wives want you to keep the maintenance up as well. So that means pluckin' those unibrows and trimming your nose hairs on a weekly basis. Oh yeah, don't forget to clip those toenails before they split your socks open. Well, then again, that might just be my toenails that do that.

As always I had had some fun with my sister. As she got up from the nest she had made in front of the couch, I shut Norwood down and gave her some love punches like only a brother could.

As I was typing up this interview, I knew it wouldn't have the same effect that my previous efforts did. Due to the fact that my sister was already taken (not to mention the fact that she's my sister), there wasn't that same fizzle of excitement as when I was talking to the other available babes. But then again, that is kind of how love is. My sister gave us some great insight into the land beyond the initial passion.

Us guys have to be extremely excited about finding our babes. I mean, God wouldn't enjoy giving us this great gift of a wife if when we encountered her we were just like, 'Ehhhh, she's alright, but I wasn't really looking forward to this anyway.' I'm sure none of us have a problem with being exhilarated about meeting the love of our life.

The problem is that we also have to be willing and ready to pursue her love even after the dazzle of that new passion fizzles and fades. We will have to choose to want to be the man she has always dreamt of even when we wake up next to her and she has bad breath.

For that reason, I think this chapter of my book serves a good purpose. It grounds us in the reality of women. After all, young girls that have not experienced a relationship without the emotional high are just as optimistic and bubbly as we are. Ok, so guys don't get bubbly, but you get the idea.

I'm not saying that we have to look at the years following marriage as the "bliss killers." But, we need not ignore the fact that our initial ecstasy will not stay forever. If we are willing to not only experience the joy of our first chance at getting to be intimate with a woman, but also to work hard to hold onto it, then we are in for one heck of a ride.

And Maria? Just so you know, you have been an inspiration to me in my life. Even though I'm your older, smarter brother, I'll definitely be modeling the way I prepare for my own marriage based on the honorable way you have handled yours. Oh, and Tom? You're not too shabby, either.

Interview Vier (4)

The Final Interview

Discovering Dating in the Midst of a Winter Wonderland

Babe Talk

Gotta have money.
Out of the 20 honnies I surveyed on whether they wanted a rich or not-so-rich guy:
15% confirmed they wanted a rich man,
25% said they favored the not-so-rich guy,
and 60% said it didn't matter.
"If he doesn't have money because he's lazy and a deadbeat than that's different."
—Stephanie W.

Discovering Dating in the Midst of a Winter Wonderland

Up to this point, I hope that I have given you some good brain food to chew on. Likewise, I am optimistic that you have gained some valuable insights from the young ladies I have been interviewing. There has definitely been an abundance of reliable advice from the girls that I myself have taken hold of.

Now, I was coming up to the sticky part of the book. I say 'sticky' because I'm currently stuck at a juncture in my life. That juncture lies at the confusing crossroads of Dating Blvd. and Not-knowing-where-to-begin St. Before I even lined up the following interview I had gained a good concept of what dating should be. I just hadn't implemented it yet.

During my experience reading about the single life I have seen advice ranging from, "Don't date," to "Date for the sake of dating." Both ideas have their merits, but what I have come up with falls somewhere between them both, favoring the latter.

I am mature enough to know that I have wasted too much time sitting still like a baby monkey waiting for 'Mama Monkey' to bring me back some berries. I am certainly willing to start climbing some trees. I'm ready to date. I understand that most books that try to discourage dating are aimed at a younger audience, and for such readers, I agree that dating is not good.

For example, I definitely didn't need to be seriously dating a girl when I was sixteen. Some would argue that dating at that age builds the characteristics and skills that such kids will need later in their dating lives. The problem is that kids that age are not looking to construct a solid dating foundation. They just want to get close to the opposite-sex and explore their curiosities. With that kind of mindset, many young kids date for the wrong reasons and thus bear bad fruit such as premarital sex. Younger daters usually end up wishing they hadn't gone as far as they had sexually. Their focus was on fulfilling their own desires, not learning good dating behavior and what they should be looking for in a companion.

On the other end of the rainbow, I recently read this book that said a person should just date to date just to get to know a person better and not to find a mate. When I told my friend Johnny about this, he spouted out, "Why don't guys just date guys then?" How true! The thing is that men and women were made to have a far deeper relationship with each other than those of the same sex ever could. So, if your desire is to get married to a beautiful woman, as I'm sure it is if you've read this far, then you have a good goal to meet. This does not mean that the first person you date will let you achieve your goal (We'll talk more about that in a second). But, it also doesn't insinuate that you shouldn't look at dating as a tool to meet your aspirations for marriage.

Dating is a stepping stone to getting married, and a really exciting one at that. But to say that you shouldn't see it as a means to finding the right person is like saying, "Climb up this ladder, but don't look where you are going." That's just stupid.

Then again, it would also be equally absurd to think that you could just jump to the fifth step of the ladder and be safe. You take one step at a time, making certain you have sure footing before stepping to the next rung.

Dating is the same. I knew that I had to get climbing and start dating. Unfortunately, many people, myself included, because of the current faux pas on dating in Christian circles, think of dating as something far more serious then it has to be. I knew that I needed to take dating more lightly in my own life. I needed to get myself out there and date some girls.

This is where my reflection from the last chapter comes into play. See, I always thought that if God was involved, I wouldn't need to make any mistakes. I would love to date, but the part that I hated even thinking about was the last word in my preceding paragraph: Girls. Plural. Scary. I didn't want to date a girl only to realize that she was the wrong one for me. After I became a Christian, I wanted to date the precise girl that I was to marry the first time. I always felt like I wasn't following God close enough if that didn't happen. This anxiety continued until one day when I pondered a certain scenario which I'll unveil in a few seconds.

Don't misunderstand me. I still get that urge to feel like I am such a scummy sinner when I make a mistake, but the following visual aid has helped me to recognize that not all mistakes are sinful. Yes, there are times when you will mess up and it's not because you are doing anything that God considers wrong. When the Bible states that we should be "perfect, even as our Father in heaven is perfect (Mt. 5:48)," it is in reference to our righteousness, not our humanness.

To exemplify, let me say that in the past I have wondered

how perfect Jesus really was. Could he have beaten me in wrestling? That is, without any angels pummeling me into the dirt, of course. A lot of times we are afraid to ask these types of questions because it tends to taint the perception of perfection we hold for our Savior. But that is our take on perfection, not God's. Even though Jesus was perfect, I'm sure he slammed his thumb with that carpenter's hammer a few times. He just never had a cussing fit afterwards. We see perfection when we look at LeBron James and see muscles surging all over his 6ft 8inch body. We see perfection when we inadvertently peek at a Victoria's Secret commercial and witness a woman's body that is the epitome of our desire. God's not so impressed with such things.

Don't forget, God crafts these traits from dust everyday. He could mold a man that could lift a thousand pounds with his tongue, from a tin can. Isn't this what John the Baptist alluded to in Matthew 3:9 when he said to the Pharisees and Sadducees, "Don't just say, 'We're safe—we're the descendants of Abraham.' That proves nothing. God can change these stones here into children of Abraham." God looks for perfection in the one thing He has given us control over: our obedience. So if God has given you the 'go ahead' to find a woman, then our sincere mess-ups are ok. (I say sincere because I'm not talking about sleeping with a girl after a few good dates and blaming it on God's permission to date.)

Ok, so here's the scenario that cleared up my perception that everybody's been waiting for: The concept of unsinful mistakes is similar, in many respects, to riding a bike. Your parents set you on your first rubber bike seat with the full premonition that you would fall down. Of course they would rather you didn't fall down and some kinesthetically gifted kids never do. But for the majority of us we all come to that point where the grass gets thick, our training wheels are wobbling and we just can't handle the speed any longer. Then BAM! CRASH! BANG! We're down crying and there's this scratch on our knee, that depending on if your mom was watching you or it was your dad, could appear to be a fatal wound or just a little war scar.

To be honest, I wrecked my bike until I was about thirteen. I remember one time when I was cruising down the sidewalk and I saw this unlevel piece of cement approaching rapidly. You know what I was thinking? Bunny Hop, baby! My little legs spun in circles like a Bugs Bunny cartoon as I readied for the stunt. As soon as my front tire left the earth everything went in slow motion

I don't really recollect exactly what happened to screw up my jump. It probably had something to do with my bike. At that time I was riding this '81 neon green Kent bicycle. The thing was ugly, but it usually rode like a champion. The paint peeling and the rubber that used to cover the handlebars being eroded away should have been my tip-off that not all was well with my Kent. That day I found out the hard way.

My bike crashed against the pavement first and my mangled body came next. I would have been alright had I not come down on the steel pipe handlebar. The oxidized shaft caught me in a very vital spot. I fell over, rolled towards the grass, and laid in the fetal position. It hurt too much to cry so I just stayed still for a few long minutes. When I was finally able to get up I was sure that I was missing part of me. If not, then I was definitely bleeding profusely. I got the courage to look down as I stretched out the elastic waist on my sweat pants. It was right in the middle of the day and I was standing next to a busy street, but I didn't care; everything was fine! Turned out I was ok after all.

Ok, I'll quit making you feel weird with my bike stories involving body parts and get back on track. So just like your parents allowed you to ride a bike knowing full well you might lose your balance and fall, God is willing to let you make some mistakes in dating. I'm not talking about mistakes you have to repent for. I'm talking about mistakes you will quickly learn from. Don't be afraid to make mistakes. Aren't you glad you know how to ride a bike now? It's the same with dating.

And don't fear that God will let you make the kind of colossal mistake that will haunt you for the rest of your days. Just like your parents knew that a scraped knee wouldn't seriously impair you, God knows what kind of dating mistakes aren't a big deal. If you are seeking God in this endeavor, He won't let you marry the wrong person. After all, your parents wouldn't let you take your bike down a steep cliff, would they? I mean, man, my mom wouldn't even have let me make that jump if I would have asked her first.

Then again, you may just ride that bike off into the sunset your first time on it. I hope so! But even if you do mess up a few dates, it's no big deal. God still loves you and He knows you'll get it right pretty soon.

My two biggest excuses that have given me the ease of mind I needed to stay far from dating have been, "I don't have the time," and, "I don't want to make a mistake." Let me expel both justifications for those of you who suffer from them as well. First, I don't have the time to deny myself dating. I can't stare at the ladder, knowing full well that I have to get to the top, but assuring myself that I don't have the time to take the first step. My excuse, that I don't have time to date, doesn't hold up very well when I look at the years that I've spent waiting for the right girl.

Secondly, not wanting to make a mistake is a noble inspiration, but it becomes a major hindrance when I use it to restrain myself from doing anything that I might make a mistake doing. I've fought this character flaw of fear of failure in other aspects in my life, so why not dating?

I'm pretty sure that you've got a good idea of what I wanted this interview to cover. I was off to ask some babes about dating, and as an added bonus, I asked the girls quite a few questions about conversation since there is a lot of that going on before, during, and after dates. Hey, I told you I would get to the conversation thing eventually.

The two girls I lined up for this interview both work with me at Family Christian Stores. The cool thing about these two ladies is how different they are. They're pretty much polar opposites. But as it turned out, many of their answers to my questions lined up perfectly.

Amy is the youngest girl I've interviewed thus far. Weighing in at only 18, you might think she's just a little high school kid. And, you'd be right. She actually goes to Elyria High, the school I've been subbing at. I've even pulled off some cool moves like going into her study hall and telling her teacher that I need to borrow her to help her with her math. Then we would go to the library and I would . . . help her with her math. Well, I guess that's not really that cool. In fact, that's just downright normal, but it made me feel cool.

Now Amy, for as long as I have known her, has been a

perplexity to me. She is very mature spiritually. Her thoughts about Christianity are pretty deep. I mean this girl is off the spiritual milk and onto the 16oz tenderloin. At school she was pulling in a 4.31 grade point average and trust me when I say she's not taking knitting 101. Try AP Calculus.

On the other hand, when it comes to social maturity, she's like a hyper little kid, which I love. One time, at the Family Christian Store, she tied my apron straps (yes, we wear purple aprons) to my manager's and when I walked away to help a customer I almost dragged my boss with me. She's always cracking me up at work as she uses her hilarious sense of humor to nail me with planned-out high-jinks.

Amy is a cutie with a tomboy mentality. I mean the girl actually challenged me to a gum spitting competition before. (Even though you'd be hard-pressed to get her to admit it, I whupped her.) Amy is definitely not your typical pretty lady. Don't get me wrong, though. She's certainly pretty and her peculiarities are very charming.

And then there was Stephanie W. I call her Stephanie W. because our company recently did some seasonal hiring and we picked up two Stephanie's. So I use the W. as a differentiating tool.

Stephanie W. carries a lot of ladylike mannerisms. She is very beautiful and looks a lot like the girl I saw in Friendly's that I thought was hot. She dresses very tastefully and that only goes to accentuate her beauty. She talks with a touch of upper class, but she seemed willing to laugh at most of my corny jokes anyway.

I haven't known Stephanie W. as long as I have Amy, but I can already tell that she has a sincere relationship with God and

CHRISTIAN BABE ALERT

it flowed through the wisdom in her well-thought-out answers.

Even though the two girls were quite different in the way they present themselves, they both got along better than fine and filled my buddy Norwood to the brim with frothy insights.

After I had done my wheeling and dealing to get both of these young ladies to agree to take some time out of their busy schedules for me, I had to set up when and where we would meet. I really wanted to try this new restaurant across the street from our ever-growing Westfield Mall, about fifteen minutes from my house. The restaurant is named Smokey Bones and it boasts a very unique look and some delicious ribs. The entrance to the bistro is covered with these rustic-looking stones that make you feel like you are going into a Fairy Tale Tavern.

Welp, I never actually made it to Smokey Bones. You see, I had to work until 10:30 the night of the interview which ended up being stretched until 11:15 and good ol' Smokey Bones was only open till 11:00. So much for taking my maidens to the castle's tavern. We ended up heading over to Denny's which happens to be open throughout the wee hours of the night.

Once we were seated in Denny's, I pulled out Norwood and two other smaller recorders that I had acquired since Norwood's little mishap with Faith and Selina. I definitely wasn't about to let that happen again. Both girls showed signs of great embarrassment as I concealed the tabletop with my family of tape-recorders. They both gave into nervous laughter as they looked around to see who was observing us. I think that the both of them thought that I was going to jot down everything they said. I mean I'm slick, but I'm not that slick.

On the plus side, by this interview I wasn't self-conscious anymore. I just slid Norwood to face my two beauties, depressed the 'record' button, and began the interview. And to Norwood's credit, he picked up the whole interview without one glitch. Ok, there was one teensy-weensy glitch. Somehow the first fifteen minutes of my interview got taped on fast speed. But, besides listening to a quarter hour of chipmunk-chat, it was all good.

When I first started the interview I could tell that Amy was a little overtaken by my recording studio so I tried to comfort her by saying, "This is how writers work, girl."

"You're not a writer," she replied with cobra-like quickness.

Ouch. But I am, too.

For my first question I just wanted to get a good idea of the expertise of the girls I had chosen concerning this particular subject matter. I asked, "How many dates—whatever you consider a date—how many dates have you guys been on?"

Amy waited a second and then said, "I don't know. A lot."

Stephanie W. chimed in immediately after Amy and agreed, "A lot."

I wanted a little more specific answer so I jokingly said, "Any number? Orrrrrr . . ."

Amy read into my sarcasm as she stated, "Four and a half times eighty." (That's 360 dates for anyone that's not good at 'mocking-math.')

Stephanie began to think of an answer as she said, "I would say, like, between . . ."

"We don't track that," Amy butted in.

"Yeah, I don't really track it," Stephanie W. continued. "It depends on what you call a date, though."

Stephanie's last statement led me to another question that could surely help us shy guys out there. I wanted to know what these girls considered an official date. One of my friends had a pretty difficult situation recently with this very thing. He had just met this girl at a youth leaders' conference and things seemed to connect (for him at least). He found out that she lived in Florida, and even though he lives in Ohio, it just so happened that he was going on a trip to Disney World with his parents in a few weeks. He kept in touch with the girl via email and eventually asked her to go to dinner with him when he got down there. He thought it was a date. She, as it turned out, didn't.

"Well, what would you guys consider a date?" I asked the girls.

"See, I would consider a date when a guy comes and asks you out and it's just you and him," Stephanie W. said. "It's not like asking you to go to a party or some kind of event where you are going to meet up. Like, when he comes and picks you up, not when you meet 'cause that's not a date."

Ahaaaa, I thought. Now that I think about it, I remember my buddy asking this girl to a few events while he was in the Sunshine State and I think they did meet up. Ok, so as much as new-age women try to convince you that dating rules have changed it seems like these godly girls still see a date as the tried and true method of a guy picking a girl up.

"Us guys need to know this stuff," I told the ladies. "We think we go on a date sometimes, but we really don't, obviously."

I was wondering what us guys should say in order to ask a girl out on a 'real' date. "Ok, number two," I said. "Give me a good line that you would like a guy to ask you out on a date with."

"I don't think you need a stupid line to ask someone out. Ya' know, just let them know you're interested," Amy began. "Be like, 'Hey, you wanna' hang out some time? Go do something?' It's not 'Hey I lost my number, can I have yours?'"

"Yeah," Stephanie W. agreed. "No lines. It's being genuine. Being just like, 'Would you like to go out sometime?'"

Amy added, "You can't just go up to a person. For me, someone can't just come up to me and be like, 'Hey, you wanna go out sometime?' I'd be like, 'No, you don't know me. Go away.'"

Stephanie W. stepped in with, "I mean it's someone, like, obviously, you've known pretty well that you've had conversations with before. But no random . . ."

"Got ya," I said. "Gotta know them. So, if you did know them for a while and it was genuine, what would you want a guy to say to you to ask you on a date? Like, give me an example of what they would say."

"I said, 'Do you wanna go hang out sometime?'" Amy sounded a little perturbed that I kept asking the same question.

"I would wanna be a little more specific," Stephanie W. jumped in. "So I would want them to be like . . . like ask for a certain day. Like, 'What are you doing this weekend?' or something. Because if they said, 'Do you wanna hang out sometime?' that leaves it too open." She then proceeded to make fun of guys leaving it up in the air as she said, "Like, 'Maybe I'll call you if I feel like it. Maybe I won't.'"

That was something that I've learned over time. Don't be weak or vague in your asking a girl to go out with you. Amy may sound like she wants a guy to ask her in a sort of formless fashion, but I'm sure that if she really liked a guy she would want him to be clear when it came to his intentions.

Girls want to know whether you're asking them to an intimate dinner-date or if you just want more people at your seven-year-old cousin's birthday party at the roller rink.

A good idea, and I know this isn't exactly a revelation, is to throw the word date in your invitation. Something like, "Hey Susie Hotsalot, would you wanna' go on a date with me this weekend?" That leaves no room for misinterpretation. Yeah, I know it's harder to say that than writing a note that says "Would you chill with me sometime before I die? Yes or No. Circle one." But trust me when I say that running around that bush will only leave you with thorns sticking in your sides.

A little while after having written this I tested out my own advice. I asked a girl out on a date. She said no. As embarrassing as that was, at least I was able to move forward and stop wondering if she liked me every time I saw her.

At this point, I realized how loud that Denny's had their 80's soft jams playing. It was actually a little disorienting.

My next question that I had in mind was something that I kind of stink at, as you'll be able to tell by how I posed my query. I'm not good at coming up with great dating destinations. Not that I've had a lot of practice, but whenever I try to wrack my brain, I usually end up with nil. And that's surprising, because I'm a pretty creative fellow. I wanted these girls to throw this old dog a few bones by means of telling me some locations that would cater to a good date.

"All right, now this is gonna help me big time because I suck at this. Give me some destinations for your fantasy dates. Like, where you would really like to go for a date," I said in kind of a demanding tone.

"My fantasy date is something completely spontaneous," Amy conferred almost immediately before jumping into a story about her ex. "Like with me and Zack; my favorite thing that we ever did was we went putt-putting and after that we were gonna go to a haunted house, but we decided not to. We went to Walmart and we went in there and we took turns picking out food products. Like peanut butter and he'd pick out the jelly. And we had a picnic in the Walmart parking lot. It was like eight at night and we went to the back of the parking lot and we just sat in the bed of my truck eating and, you know, just talking. And that was my favorite thing that we ever did. It was amazing! Completely spontaneous. Random."

'Hmmph,' I thought. That was definitely different than the seven course meal I had envisioned at the most expensive restaurant I could imagine. Before passing judgment I had to see what Stephanie W. had to say about the issue.

"What do you have to say, Miss W.?" I said.

"Miss W.," Stephanie W., began, repeating what I had just said as she pondered the question. "Ummm, I think it definitely has to be spontaneous. It's not . . . It never has to be something where it involves a lot of money or anything, I don't think. It's just more like—I don't know—Well, like, some of my favorite times have been just like getting in the car and driving downtown." (I think Miss. W. may have been referring to downtown Cleveland.) "Stopping at Edgewater Park and sitting on the rocks," she went on. "You know, that's fun. Getting ice cream. Just sitting there."

Wow, it was true. The way that I would have created a fantasy date for these girls, had I gone out with either of them, would have been drastically different. And I'm sure a lot of you guys think along the same lines I do. I admitted this to them as I said, "That's a good point. That's a really good point. See, us guys don't understand that. I mean, I kinda knew that in the back of my head, but not really. See, the way us guys think is the more money, the more fancy, the better. But, obviously, that's not true."

Later, after I had let this thought of 'poverty dating' stew in my brain for about a week It all began to make sense. The first connection I made was when I thought about my mom. She used to love it when my dad would take her for drives in Cleveland. Cleveland is a pretty largely populated city of about 500,000. It has a gorgeous night skyline—for a small city boy like me—and some crazy traffic due to way too many one-way streets.

Since my dad started acting like a bum by neglecting my mom I've had the privilege of taking her for drives once in a while. Don't get me wrong, I enjoy doing it. It's just that my mom's a little strange about where she likes to drive in Cleveland. She relishes driving through the bad parts of Cleveland and I'm sure that Cleveland's reputation has preceded me in telling you that it contains some pretty rough parts of town.

I think women just like that thrill of being somewhere dangerous with a guy to protect them. Sorry Mom, but if we get in trouble on the East side, I'm gonna run. Just kidding . . . a little.

The more I thought about it, the more I recognized that a great date involves doing something memorable, and not necessarily monetary. I mean, a lot of times things cost money. Geez, parking your car in Cleveland costs two toes. But, don't restrict your thinking to only the things that take a lot of money. We dudes seem to be tricked by all of the diamond ads we see these days. They seem to sum up the philosophy of our modern culture: In order to impress a girl you need to spend big. Just take a gander at some of those goofy lookin', secular rap artists driving around their too-big-for-life Hummer H7's. They would impress upon us that we need to splurge on everything in order to impress young ladies.

Let me tell you straight: The only way you'll always need to spend big is if your character isn't so big. A godly woman would rather have you be a good listener and be thoughtful than find roses at her door every day for the rest of her life. She would rather have you be faithful to her instead of having a diamond that blinds the neighbors every time the sun comes up.

I'm not sure how I got off on that tangent, but the point I learned is simple. Girls want you more than your stuff. This goes hand in hand with the awesome verse that Paul says in 2 Corinthians 12:14. He says, "I don't want what you have; I want you." Learn to make your dates focus around her and you rather than being drowned out by the surroundings. And you know as well as I do that doesn't mean, 'Don't spend money on your girl.' It means, 'Don't let money be the focus.'

I thought Amy's idea about Walmart was out of this world. Who would have thought about that? (Besides Amy and Zack.) And if you're not hungry, buy a loaf of bread and toss it to the seagulls in the parking lot.

Right about this time, as I was transitioning to my next question, our waitress arrived on the scene with a circular tray in hand. The waitress then proceeded to set my 'Moons Over My Hammy' down in front of me. I took a reasonable sized bite as Amy and Stephanie W. were served and almost immediately thereafter recoiled back into the interview.

With some cheesy eggs still melting between my teeth I said, "Ok, should guys always pay for the dates?"

"No," Amy said without a moment's notice.

"No?" I said inquisitively, wondering if Amy had heard my question correctly. "Why not?"

Amy responded by saying, "It makes it too formal. It freaks me out. Me personally. Every once in a while with me and Zack; he'd let me pay sometimes. Or just for my stuff at least. And, like, with that one date at Walmart, I mean, we split the price right in half and it was fun. We didn't have to worry about anything."

Stephanie W. had a little bit of a difference in opinion as she divulged, "I think that if you are . . . If a guy asks you on a date then he should pay. I think if you're in a relationship where you are dating exclusively then it can kind of, like, be shared. Like . . . You know . . . Yeah!"

"Ok, that makes sense," I said still chomping on my food.

My next uncertainty involved touchy, feely stuff. You know that as guys we want to be as physically close to our babes as, well . . . physically possible. We love the "arm candy." That is, having a beautiful girl pulled close to you so everyone can see that she's yours. But then there's that little problem of not knowing when to make the move "in." It's kind of like watching a basketball player outside the foul line. Great players dribble with their back to the rim and, suddenly, at the right moment, when the defenses' guard is down, the player bursts to the hoop for the slam! I remembered how Faith and Selina had told me that when I went for moves like the arm-around-the-shoulder tactic, I had to be confident just like that b-ball player.

I needed to know what was good for a first date so that I could have that confidence. "How close should a guy on the first date get? You know, like the arm-around-the-shoulder? Stuff like that," I pried.

"He shouldn't do anything," Stephanie W. admitted.

"Not close at all?" I said with surprise.

"Not at all," Stephanie W. reiterated.

As both of the girls nodded their heads with approval, I conceded, "That's unanimous. Ok, gotcha. Stay away."

Amy laughed as she said, "He said, 'Stay away.'"

But I just couldn't leave it at that so I said, "So like what is the distance? Like if you're walking just stay distant? Like forty or fifty feet or something?"

Stephanie W. deciphered my sarcasm with a giggle. "Just, no, don't try to grab a hand or anything. None of that."

Amy said, "Like you would a friend. You're not gonna be like hugging a friend walking down the mall. Normal distance. Everyone has personal bubble space."

I understood what these ladies were getting at. Touching a girl should be special. The first time you hold her hand should be something to wait for. I know it sounds like a loaf of cornbread, but it's true. There is this verse in Proverbs that states if you have a word from God, you can wait your turn to speak it. It's a similar premise here. If you feel an uncontrollable urge to be all over a girl the first hour that you are out with her then it's not from God. Now, the urge to touch a girl—and smell her hair and wrap her up in your strong arms—is from God.

I'm sure you've heard before that our God is a God of order

as in 1 Corinthians 14:33.

This indicates that He doesn't do things in the heat of the moment. That doesn't insinuate that God isn't moved by passion for us. But just that He always withholds His actions until the time is right, regardless of the passion burning inside of Him.

Think about when you got saved. If you guys were like me, then you wasted a lot of time doing stupid stuff before God really broke into your life. For me, it seems like God could have made His moves on me a lot earlier in order to prevent me from doing all of the stupid things that I did. I mean, I know God has had a fiery desire to see me saved even before time began. So why did He wait for me? Because the time wasn't right before that. I wasn't ready. Not that God wasn't ready. God loved me so much that He waited for me to get there.

I know it seems kind of crazy to compare God's saving works to holding a girl's hand at the mall, but the analogy actually works in our favor. If God can hold back His great and mighty passion to see you saved until you are ready for Him to move in, then certainly us guys can withhold from getting too close to a girl on the first date. And, hey, it might not be what all Christian women want, but we just had two of them tell us that it was what they wanted.

So much for the silky smooth moves I was planning for date numero uno. Just kidding. I've got no moves. That actually relieves some of the pressure. Knowing that a girl actually wishes I would stay a friend's distance away on a first date makes my life a little easier.

My next question was just for me. Maybe a few of you messier fellas can relate. "When a guy comes to pick you up, how much does it matter that he has a clean car?" I questioned.

"What?" Amy said with an odd fury in her voice.

"I'm sorry. It's a question," I said with a scared little boy's laugh.

At that point Amy and Stephanie W. both began to speak at the same time and it sounded like some gibberish from an Ewok out of Star Wars.

"I don't think it should be, like, growing fungus on the floor," Amy said a little louder than Stephanie W.'s, "It matters! It matters."

Whoa! Better clean up the algae-coated interior in my 'Datemobile,' I thought.

Stephanie W. continued as she said, "Because your car says a lot. If you have a messy car it means you have a messy house, which means you don't take care of yourself and you don't take care of your possessions and you're a slob."

As Stephanie and I laughed off her abrupt explosion of hatred for dirty dudes, I said, "Oh my gosh . . . I better clean my freakin' car!"

"I don't mind a little clutter, but just filth . . . No way," Stephanie concluded.

I calmed down my laughter and looked at Amy. "So what do you think? Just no fungus?" I said.

"No fungus or food," Amy added. "You can have tools and stuff in your truck or your car or whatever."

"In fairness, I grew up in a really neat freak family so . . .," Stephanie included, to try to soften her white-glove viewpoint.

"My mom's like Adam," Amy said. (*Don't worry, I'll explain who Adam is in a second.*) "Organization is key for me but it doesn't have to be. Maybe that's not someone's strong point. It's not like that's who they are, you know."

"I guess that they can be portrayed to be kind of lazy sometimes. Like that's how I kinda look at things . . . Just, you know, clean. Don't be lazy," Stephanie summed up.

"Gotcha," I said. "Clean the car, guys. You bunch of lazy bums!" (Whisper: Please don't be mad, guys. I just had to pretend like I was on her side.)

Since Amy's comment necessitates an explanation of who Adam is, you better get ready for those 'going back in the past' swirlies like you see on TV shows. I'm taking you back to a point in the distant past. A time when I still wet the bed. Ok, maybe not that far back, but close.

About two years ago, when I was at work at Family Christian Stores, in walked this tall stranger. His wavy red locks drooped past his chin. He looked like a California surf boy. When he spoke he had all of the 'Whoa, dude' mannerisms to match his appearance. To my great surprise this young bro wanted a job.

He was a little freaky, but I loved his energy so I put in a good word for him and he got the job. To make a long story a little longer, I'll mention that after Adam got hired we used to do some pretty goofy stuff. In fact, when we weren't taking care of customers we were always messing around with anything we could get our hands on.

Then, one fateful day, Adam got promoted to 'senior sales.' Soon thereafter, Adam's OCD began to surface. He was a clean freak. And just to relay the degree of his clean freakishness, I am compelled to tell the following story:

Our store had just gotten a new manager named Damian. He was the best manager I had seen in my entire six years of retail, and I've had some good managers. But Damian loved to play evil little tricks abusing my need to have fun. One particular work day, Adam was obsessively occupied with organizing our Bible cover section. Damian walked up to innocent old me (picture me with Bambi eyes if you will) and said, 'I dare you to take this Bible cover and go shove it in the covers Adam already fixed.' As the large cover bobbed in Damian's hand, I knew I was being tempted, but I couldn't fight it. I grabbed the denim-like cover and headed towards my victim.

Adam was working so non-stop he scarcely noticed me. I began to pry the cover in sideways between a row of neatly placed, vertical covers. Adam looked up, astonished, and asked, 'Dan, what're you doing?'

I didn't say a word.

As I just kept thrusting the cover into the spot into which it would not fit, Adam repeated his question with more fervor. 'Dan! What're you doing?'

At that time I gathered together all of the fake sincerity I had and said, "I'm just trying to help you, Adam."

Then I walked away to get another Bible cover to shove into place, but I guess Adam was onto me. As I turned back towards him again, I saw a huge, leather cover whirling through the air. Adam looked like an insane lumberjack hurling his trusty axe. In a split-second's time, the cover smashed me in the groin. I fell to the ground, in the middle of the bookstore, wondering what on a Bible cover could've possibly hurt me so badly! Later, I realized that it was the cover's gigantic brass zipper head that had done the damage. Damian came up to me and said in a stunned voice, 'Dan! Why were you bothering Adam? He was working so hard on that!'

For my next question, I wanted to burst into the topic of "conversation." Conversation is hardly a natural feeling when you first meet a girl. I wanted to get us guys some insider tips on what women enjoy talking about so that we could be one step ahead of the game. Rather than fumbling for our words like tranquilized baboons, we could have a good idea of what we might want to talk about.

But, before I even get back to the interview I want to bestow upon you some of my own insights on the subject. Number one: make her the center of attention. Don't let your interest in her waver or sway.

By that, I mean if you are eating in a restaurant don't keep looking at the door to see who just came in and whether or not you know them. Let her know just by your focus that you're not there for anyone else but her. If one of your friends does happen to wander into where the two of you are then make your greeting swift and sweet. Never, I repeat never, stand there socializing with someone you know at the cost of your date feeling left out.

Just recently this super nice guy I met at church, named Jeremy, showed me just how this works. Jeremy is actually Selina's cousin and he used to light up every time I would see him. He would shake my hand and give me a hug with a huge smile on his face. But the last time I said something to him at church, he wasn't alone. He was there with his newfound babe. Surprisingly, when I talked to him in the church hallway, he cut me short with a quick reply. Now if I hadn't known that he was waiting to walk his woman out, I might have been offended. But in all truthfulness it was cool. He was showing me exactly where I stood on the totem pole of love and I would expect no less from any strong man.

Secondly, when it comes to conversation, get interested in your woman. Don't be so concerned with impressing her. If you are going to marry this girl, you better spend some time finding out about her. One little trick I read at a seminar at my church was to pay more attention to what she is saying rather than what you are going to say next.

We all know what that's like. Have you ever met someone that you wanted to impress but before you finished shaking their hand you forgot what they just said their name was? It was because you were using all of your brain reserve to try to think of a witty remark that would make an impression on them rather than listening to what they were saying.

I took a big ol' swig of pop and as I pulled the glass from my lips, ice cubes still jingling, I said, "Once you're on a date and go to a good place, what are some good topics of conversation that guys can start with?"

"Church," Amy said in her cut-to-the-point kind of fashion.

"Church? Like, what about church?" I probed.

"Just what's going on in their church or their walk with God," Amy clarified.

Stephanie W. fell right in with Amy's answer as she said, "Yeah. God's, I think, one of the best things to always discuss. 'Cause I think it's important to know where someone stands before you ever go further. Even on a second date or anything you need to know where they stand."

"And with me," Amy started in, "I really won't even so much allow myself to go on the date unless I know where they stand on that. So, even before that, it's a conversation matter. That's my personal conviction that I won't do that unless they are strong with God because, you know, if that goes on to something more serious he needs to have that basis and he needs to be able to stand for God. Even if that means putting me down sometimes. And that's important to me. That he can put God before me."

Stephanie W. said, "Yeah," agreeing with Amy's stance.

"Good point," I said. "Give me one more topic."

After a few moments of silence I said, "Something that you would like a guy to talk to you about. Ask you about."

Stephanie W. then voiced up. "Umm, it sounds stupid, but I guess it's nice to talk to a guy about what he thinks about dating and stuff. It's interesting. Even when you're out on a date, it's just interesting to like hear their . . . Not experiences, but just their thoughts I guess."

"Heck, yeah," I said.

"Family," Amy threw out there. "You know. They have to be interested in what's going on in my family's life and, you know, I like to be interested in what's going on in their family. Because you're not just gonna like them. You're gonna like their family."

Ok, there were three great topics of discussion for you guys. God, dating, and family. Basically, start thinking about areas of interest you have in those topics and come up with some great questions to ask.

For my following question, I already had a predetermined answer that was supposed to just flow out of these women's lips as soon as I said my part. I was in no way expecting the response I ended up getting even though it essentially made perfect sense.

"How important, like in the beginning stages of dating, how

important is conversation? I mean should there be a lot of conversation?" I asked my two ladies.

"There should always be a lot of conversation," Amy replied.

Ok, that was the point I expected, just like I anticipate the light at the end of my road to always turn red on me. It was bound to happen. And for good reason. Most of us know that it's a good idea to talk a lot to someone you want to get to know. The next thing the girls brought to my attention was the unforeseen part.

Stephanie W. replied, "I think that there should be . . . You should always be careful of where your conversation goes. And too much conversation can go . . . well, there's certain extents where your conversation shouldn't go. And by talking a lot that could happen."

"That's a good point," I said. "Yeah, that happens to me a lot."

"Where you get that like, high note," Stephanie W. proceeded. "It's like an emotional attachment by just knowing a lot about each other. I guess too much detail sometimes isn't good."

"Gotta have, like, boundaries," I suggested.

"Yeah, definitely," Stephanie half-whispered.

Amy then added, "You should always talk about what your boundaries are. And that should always be a reminder in the conversation. In how you present yourself and what you say."

"Cool! Good stuff, ladies," I voiced energetically.

There have been some times that I have gotten so caught up in the fact that girls like to talk that I dove in a little too deep. I was trying to find Nemo, if you will, forgetting that I couldn't breathe underwater.

For example, it's remarkable how much the Bible says in so short a verse. Steal a look at Proverbs 10:19 with me. The New Living Translation reads like this, "Don't talk so much, for it fosters sin. Be sensible and turn off the flow!"

Wow! That's pretty powerful. There are plenty of times in my life where I've had to "turn off the flow." I remember this one girl at college that I happened to sit next to the first day of class. She was quite soothing on the eyes. And it ended up she enjoyed my sense of humor too!

We talked every day we had class and I got more and more, as Stephanie W. so gracefully put it, "emotionally attached" to her. That is, until about five weeks into the class, when the girl told me she was engaged and pregnant. Talk about, "Ouch!"

But even back then I lived by the principle of guarding how deeply I got involved. Even with this girl I was fairly protective of how intimate our conversations got because I pretty much knew she didn't know Jesus. Still, the power of our conversations attracted me to her regardless. After she gave me her little surprise news about having a fiancée and whatnot, I had to be even more careful about what I said.

I remember there being times when I would feel like the biggest loser because I would prohibit myself from talking to her about certain things. One thing that made me feel especially bad was when she talked about problems she was having with her soon-to-be hubby. I felt so bad just letting this sad girl sit there when I could have comforted her. Don't get me wrong. She wasn't the type of girl to start weeping as she laid all of her problems on the table. But, just by the process of time and through the channel of our friendship things came out. I remember driving home crying once in awhile due to the fact that my emotions were so tangled up. I knew I didn't really want her and, in fact, I couldn't have her, but I was no less bonded with her.

In the end, I did what was right and slowly drifted away from our conversations. It was hard and I hated it, but I guarantee it was the only saving move. You might say, "Well, she was taken and pregnant and not even a Christian. The girl I'm talking to isn't any of that." True, but you still don't know if you're gonna marry someone right away. So be careful and make boundaries for yourself.

Let me give you an example that involves me talking with my one Christian buddy. He is a lot closer to marriage than I am and a lot more comfortable talking about sexual things than I am. Now, he's not a pervert, but chatting about intimate times with a girl hits me a heck of a lot harder than it does him. So, whenever we have been talking a while and the conversation strolls down that scary alley, I have to tighten up a little. My buddy doesn't know how much I can take so he sometimes unintentionally keeps yappin'. At those times I usually just say, "Awww, man, I don't want to talk about that." That's usually all it takes. I know what I can handle and I set up boundaries accordingly.

Now, just knowing your boundaries is a good first step, like on G.I. Joe how they used to say, "Knowing is half the battle." Then again, there'll be times when you know the conversation shouldn't go any further but you just let it slide on by. For me, I wouldn't even talk about anything regarding sex with a girl I was on a first date with, except for the fact that it should be preserved until after marriage. Not because I'm a prude freak or because I think it's gross, but because from that point on thoughts will be entering my head that are way too hard to control.

You know how the Bible says that we should be "bringing into captivity every thought to the obedience of Christ (2 Cor. 10:5, KJV)." Well, I don't like the idea of letting my thoughts gain the power of a rabid werewolf before trying to bring them into captivity. I'd rather catch them and tame them while they are still guinea pigs. The best way to do that is to have set barriers for conversation and not cross them, no matter how intriguing it might seem.

"Ok, next one," I said. "A lot of times on a date with a guy there's those awkward silent moments. Are those always a bad thing?"

"No," Stephanie W. said.

"Why not?" I said, imploring Stephanie W. to continue.

Stephanie W. took my hint as she said, "I think it's very . . . I don't know why actually. I used to have this big problem with awkward silences 'cause I always felt like I should be talking. I'd be like, 'Um, so anyways, like . . . You know?' And the one guy I was talking to, um, he's like, 'You know you don't—when there is like an awkward silence—just don't say anything.' He's like, 'Just let it be.' It's good to have that because you know that it's . . . I don't know . . . I can't explain it. I just think it's good. I think it says something."

"Silence says something," I said in a news flash kind of tone as I began to laugh.

Amy spoke into Mr. Norwood, saying, "We're out here to confuse you guys. That's what this is."

"It does. It does," Stephanie W. kept saying.

"Yeah i-i-it does," I said in a broken stutter. I knew what she was saying, but I just couldn't form my words quick enough. "It definitely can show if you are comfortable with somebody."

"I think it shows confidence if you can just sit there," Amy said one-upping my response.

"Yeah, that's true," Stephanie W. concurred.

"I think it makes it adventurous, spontaneous, random. That's what I'm about. Randomosity," Amy maintained.

"I know. You're a random, crazy woman," I said, for what reason I'm not completely sure.

At that time, Stephanie W.'s vibrant eyes shifted upwards as she said, "I love this song."

The song was foreign to me. And it sounded kinda creepy. I played along in order to not upset her eerie music mood.

"Ok, this is just a quick one," I said

"No," Amy butted in.

I could sense we were getting a little slap happy so I decided to finish up soon. After all, it was getting pretty late. "What is one thing you would look for in a first date that would show you that you would want to go onto another date?"

After about 10 seconds of nothingness I said, "One of these silent times. I'm showing I'm confident."

The girls and I let off a few boisterous laughs before Stephanie W. finally said, "I haven't had a lot of good dates."

After some more goofy banter I did get a little information out of the young ladies. In compressed MP3 format it came out as follows: If the date was comfortable through and through and if the guy does the little gestures (such as opening car doors) that show he is trying, then a second date would be in order.

For my second to last question with these two beauties I said, "Can you guys . . . You ladies, give guys any advice about stuff that they should do differently on dates? Like you said, you've had some crappy dates," I said, addressing Stephanie W. "What stuff should they do different that they never seem to think of?"

"Relax," Amy said with a melting ice cube in her mouth.

"Thank you," I said.

"Does that count?" Amy asked.

I started cracking up as I said, "Yeah, it counts," but I couldn't stop myself from a little mockery. "No, that one doesn't count, Amy. Next!"

As the girls and I had another laugh with a side of stomach pains, I had to move on. But Amy had one more idea. She said, "Don't try to be tough. I have a thing for tough guys, but when they try to be that way I'm like, 'Shut your face!'"

I did have another question, but the clock hands were well past the midnight hour and my Pumpkin-mobile was waiting outside. Yet, there was still one more important detail the girls brought to my attention in the midst of our Coca-Cola caffeine drunkenness.

When I tried to ask the ladies about a good way to end a first date, they could hardly respond without shooting their drinks from their noses. Ahh, the pains of late-night interviews. But they did communicate to me that they struggled with the guys ending it with the phrase, "Hey, I'll give you a call." Stephanie W. said she wanted them to call, but that empty promise often left her anxious and worried, not knowing when or if the guy would follow through.

I told the girls that I could empathize because I have a

similar, but somewhat different experience every morning. I said, "It's like when I have to get up for subbing in the morning. Same thing. They have to call me if they need me to sub at a particular school. And I need work. I need money. But as soon as I get up in the morning at 5:45 AM, I hope they don't call me. I'm like, 'Oh, please don't call me. Please just let me go back to bed.' I sit there for about an hour straight. I'm thinking, 'Please don't call me,' as I'm getting ready, ironing my clothes. Then the phone will be like, 'Rrrrring.' I'll be like, 'I hate you.'"

Well, I guess us guys should be more specific with the call back info. Try saying, "Hey, can I call you tomorrow at about seven?" After all, waiting for the unknown is the killer.

With that, I packed up my trusty tape recorder, tossed down the tip, and we headed out.

As the ladies and I walked outside, we noticed that the ground had been candy-coated with a decently thick sheet of snow. The snow was still falling on the pure white parking lot. The moonlight reflected off of the snowflakes, creating an illusive radiance. It was really pretty magical.

But I couldn't let one of my interviews end on such a tranquil note, so I reached down and cupped some snow. It was good packing snow, but my stooping was enough to lure the girls into a wintry fight. Sadly for Amy and Stephanie W., they both threw like girls.

After our snowball fight, we said our goodbyes and headed to our vehicles that all looked as if they were owned by snowmen. We scraped our windows, calmed down a little and drove off.

I was amazed at the snowfall that our little city had received during our midnight meeting. It was so slippery that I almost hit Stephanie W.'s car on the way out of the parking lot. That would've been a bad way to thank her for her time.

As I drove home, I flipped my Explorer into 4 wheel drive, and fishtailed nearly the whole way back. Sorry, mom, I couldn't help it. Not a car in sight. Blinking yellow lights. It was like God was saying, "You finished your interviews, son, go ahead and celebrate!"

Once again, I was pleasantly enlightened by the time I got to spend with some Christian babes. I'm planning on trying out their advice on dating and conversation very soon.

The unblemished gem that I took away from this interview was to not get pulled into commercial romance when dating.

It's actually a little bizarre because last night, as soon as I had finished typing the previous sentence onto the computer screen, I decided to call it a night. At that point, I began to close everything out. Right as I was moving my fidgety arrow to the 'x' on my web browser, I noticed a curious topic lining the top of the home page. It said something to the effect of, "10 worst holiday commercials." I then checked the image directly below the caption. It showed a flawless looking guy handing a gorgeous girl a present as they both smiled like a couple of mushy goofs.

After scanning the article a little, I found out that the commercial was supposedly trying to show the blissful emotions experienced by giving an expensive gift. I guess it failed to do so since it was thrown into the fireplace with nine other "worst holiday" commercials.

I just thought it was neat to see that some people are actually catching on to the fact that "most expensive" doesn't always equal "best." In fact, just the other day I heard that because Americans tend to naturally equate expense with quality, an ice cream brand took advantage of it. The frosty dessert manufacturer decided to overprice their product in order to make people think it was the highest quality on the market. So you ended up getting run-of-the-mill soft serve in a fancy box for an outrageous price, all the while thinking you were experiencing the best that the world of frozen delicacies had to offer. And, even funnier, it worked!

I'm positive that this tricky treat was not the first item to be overpriced for the sole sake of cunning quality manipulation. And it is all right to be fooled once in a while. After all, you may have just wanted some super rich ice cream. But don't let this ideal that more money always leads to more happiness fool you.

To illustrate this point, take a glimpse at the *Song of Solomon* in the Bible. Solomon and his babe were infatuated with each other. I mean this book is loaded with some stirring love talk. And as you read you'll scarcely notice a mention of Solomon's wealth. And Solomon was rich!

Later in Solomon's life, the Bible states in 1 Kings 10:14, "Each year Solomon received about 666 talents of gold. This did not include the additional revenue he received from merchants and traders, all the kings of Arabia, and the governors of the land." So let's try that again in modern day terms. The 666 talents of gold would be equivalent to 23 metric tons or roughly 25 standard tons. The price of gold, as of me writing this, is just above $1,580 per ounce. Since there is 16 ounces in a pound and 2000 pounds in a ton . . . (I'll give you a few minutes . . .) That means that Solomon was pulling in more

CHRISTIAN BABE ALERT

than 1.26 billion dollars a year in gold alone. Sorry, but Bill Gates is like a poor little orphan boy when compared to Solomon. (Okay, so I took it one step too far.)

Regardless of your appreciation for math, Solomon was kind of wealthy. Of course, there are some factors that I didn't account for in determining just how wealthy, but you get the point. Despite this wealth, in his "love journal" you don't see the two lovers focusing on the money. Rather, they are completely absorbed with each other.

That is how dating should be. Don't take it to the extremes of Solomon right away, of course. These two songbirds had just gotten married after all, so don't quote the book on your first date saying, "Your breasts are like twin fawns of a gazelle, feeding among the lilies." And for the sake of modern hygiene don't ever quote things like, "Your teeth are as white as newly washed sheep. They are perfectly matched; not one is missing." Some of these phrases just worked better back then. Then again you would do well to keep quotes like this in mind: "Look away, for your eyes overcome me! (Song of Solomon 6:5)."

When you plan for a date, remember to make wherever you go or whatever you do accentuate the two of you and not the other way around. Check out this quote from the *Song of Solomon* to see what I mean. "How lovely are your cheeks with your earrings setting them afire! How stately is your neck, accented with a long string of jewels."

Notice how this girl most likely wore some impressive jewelry, yet Solomon only saw it as means to draw attention to her natural assets. When you go on a date or give a gift, think about your lady more than the gift or location. Everyone can save for a few weeks and take a girl to a fancy restaurant, but not everyone can take a girl where you can.

For instance, almost everyone around where I live could tell you where an Olive Garden is but I'm probably one of a very select group of guys that could tell you where you should go in the park this time of year. Where the snow lies undisturbed, and the fallen trees make for a mystical backdrop. Where the only sound you'll hear is the crunch of the leaves covered in snow beneath your feet. And I'm not telling where it is, either. What if a guy from Elyria reads this? I would be done for.

The point is that you are unique and in being so you have a God-given advantage over other guys. If you like to fish . . . Well, don't take her fishing and make her put the worm on the hook. That's just sick. But I bet you know exactly where a still pond is settled. I would even lay a wager that you would know the best bank on which to set a picnic basket.

My point is that you don't always need the bright lights and rubbing elbows with uptown folks that money affords you. It's nice sometimes, but using a little creativity will payoff better most of the time.

After thinking a million thoughts, I finally pulled into my driveway sometime around one in the morning. The snow was still drifting from the sky, and knowing that this was my last interview I couldn't help but just thank God for letting me get to do it all. I walked up my steps, opened my door and headed off to bed.

BABES BEWARE!

Good stuff! That's pretty much all there is to it. We extracted just about as much wisdom, insight, and common sense involving the inner workings of the Babe Machine as we will need. We let nine fine specimens of the hot, Christian, babe genus talk our ears off for a good while. And I know you guys pulled some golden nuggets out of the rivers of feedback we received.

If you are anything like me, than you more than likely already knew a portion of what such God-crafted ladies were looking for. But, it's awesome to uncover some new intricacies while at the same time reassuring yourself of what you already knew. And remember, I'm just human. So, if you ended up disagreeing with me on some small point, feel free to treat what I said like a chicken nugget. You know how chicken nuggets are good for the most part, but once in a while you end up chewing on some inedible piece of gristle and you have to spit it out. Just don't toss the whole nugget. After all, there's some good meat in there, man. (The unknown white meat.)

This book was intended first and foremost to . . . Get me a Christian babe. Secondly, I wanted everyone reading it to find some 'universal traits' about Christian women that, although seemingly insignificant, can change your whole game. I want us Christian guys to understand these girls so that we can get dates and more importantly transform into some legendary husbands (at least in our wives' and God's eyes).

Just as I began this book depicting the dual-layered road that we must walk, by flipping to the pages of Abraham and Isaac, I'm going to finish up on a similar note. Remember that there are basically two objectives when it comes to finding our babe. (This'll be familiar to any of you guys that ever had the indulgence of playing through the objective-based magnificence that was GoldenEye on the Nintendo 64.)

Objective one: we have to be prepared to meet our babe by having a stockpile of inside information. That is what I hope this book supplied you with. I want you and I to be filled with awe-inspiring knowledge about girls. The kind of knowledge that, when put into action, will dazzle the girls we find and set us far apart from the average Joe-hubby.

Objective two: I want us to be fully ready and willing to put it into practice. So, I not only want you to have an armload of ammunition, but I want you to know how to load the guns and fire. I hope this book has encouraged you and motivated you enough to get you moving in the right direction.

I can say that this book has assuredly helped me in both respects. Primarily I've been boosted dramatically in my awareness of what Christian women desire. Secondly, I've been constantly evolving in my willingness to use my expertise. (Don't you hate when people use the word evolution? Just know that I'm not talking about the comic-book-like idea that men came from a long extinct variety of apes.)

What I mean by evolving is that I have been consistently

changing for the better ever since I put my first couple thousand words on the monitor. And the amazing part is that, for the most part, it hasn't been my idea to alter my willingness to move on in my quest for my lady.

It's almost comical to me how many times God has subtly tested me with this book. From dusting to dating, God has let me know that I've got to practice what I preach. Just last Sunday I went to church with the half-intention of asking this blonde-haired babe out to lunch. I say half-intention, because although I prepped myself to ask her out (bought a new, sexy shirt, trimmed all facial fur, and left my house early) I still wasn't all together in the willingness department. Hey, I'm still working on it. Luckily, I mean, regrettably she wasn't there.

The cool thing is that this book has helped me to have a much more optimistic approach to finding my babe. Talking to these nine girls has encouraged me to work on my willingness more aggressively until I'm finally ready to roll. (So I will be asking this girl at my church out very soon. If this book happens to get published magically fast, then pray for me. Oh, pray for me anyway, and I'll be praying for all of you guys too.)

Ok, so I said that the first two objectives consisted of getting prepared and willing. And that is what I look forward to this book doing for you as it has for me. The final objective, should you choose to accept it, is to let God do His thing. I know that the world will tell you that knowing what you are doing and being able to do it are all you will need, but the Bible tells us a different story.

If you would take a look at Psalm 33 with me. Starting at verse 16 the Bible says, 'The best equipped army cannot save a king, nor is great strength enough to save a warrior. Don't count on your warhorse to give you victory—for all its strength, it cannot save you. But the Lord watches over those who fear him, those who rely on his unfailing love.' Then in verse 20 it states, 'We put our hope in the Lord. He is our help and our shield. In him our hearts rejoice, for we trust in his holy name.'

Let me restate this in babe lingo. 'The best-looking guy cannot save a marriage, nor are great looks enough to save a relationship. Don't count on your new, V8 Mustang (you can substitute manners, charm, or skill for 'new, V8 Mustang') to give you victory–for all its appeal, it cannot get the right girl.'

The rest of the verse works pretty well as is.

Does that mean warriors like David and Samson were not strong or skilled? Absolutely not! Listen to what David said in 1 Samuel 17:34. 'When a lion or a bear comes to steal a lamb from the flock, I go after it with a club and take the lamb from its mouth. If the animal turns on me, I catch it by the jaw and club it to death.' David was one freaky kid. And we all know the exploits of Samson. So obviously these were a couple of strong, skillful dudes. But that alone wasn't what made them able to fight successfully. They were conquerors because they understood the duality of tuning their skills but relying on God to point out how to best use them.

And if you are still not convinced that God will touch your heart when the time comes to move in for a particular girl then let me offer one more verse. I know it seems like it's Bible reading time at your local library, but I'm sure some of you still feel like you will have to find your girl relying solely on skill and charm because God doesn't move us to do things so trivial.

Let me present you with a story from the book of Ezra. 'In the first year of king Cyrus of Persia, the Lord fulfilled the

CHRISTIAN BABE ALERT

prophecy he had given through Jeremiah,' the first chapter begins. About three-quarters of a century earlier God had told Jeremiah that because the Israelites were downright wicked, He would let them be carried off to Babylon as captives. Then 70 years later God would bring back his chosen people to Jerusalem. The book of Ezra picks up at God's appointed time for His children to travel back home from their exile.

As verse one of Ezra continues it says that God 'stirred the heart of Cyrus'. God basically moved on Cyrus' heart to send the last remnant of Israel back to build the temple at Jerusalem, which was in Judah. Then in the fifth verse it says, 'Then God stirred the hearts of the priests and Levites and the leaders of the tribes of Judah and Benjamin to go to Jerusalem to rebuild the temple of the Lord.

God works the same way today! He stirs hearts. He may not shake yours up until it's a bloody slushy, but He will move you exactly enough to let you know that it is Him.

And finally, if you are still wondering if God would go through all of this crazy amount of trouble to get you to the girl that He meant for you to become one with, then listen carefully to what I'm about to say next. OH YEAH HE WOULD!

I told you about how He did it for Isaac, Abraham's son. And He'll do it for you too. Why? Because as the lyrical psalmist David put it in Psalm 32:8, 'The Lord says, 'I will guide you along the best pathway for your life' (NLT). Not a nice pathway. Not a comfortable and fairly-sought-after pathway. But the absolute *best* pathway.

She is out there and you will find her. And she will truly love you. Although I love you, too, I pray that this book has readied you because I can't possibly type one more word.

Post Story

Wow! Here I am, at age 33. It's kind of funny because I remember being younger and thinking, "Dang, 30 is so old!" Now, it's just kind of normal. I mean, I still play video games . . . a lot. You could probably even catch me eating out with my buddies at some of the same old restaurants. It amazes me to see how time goes on, and so many parts of life remain the same.

    I guess one big difference is that I now have a hot babe sitting beside me. OH YEAH! I forgot to mention that I finally got married about two years after I finished this book (And, no, it wasn't one of the ladies I interviewed.)

    I will tell you that finding my lovely wife is the best blessing that has happened to me since meeting Jesus when I was 16. I have fond memories of being a brand-spanking-new baby Christian, thinking God was going to let me meet my soul mate within a month or two of deciding to follow Him. I was actually praying that God would let this pretty girl down the street fall in love with me. Little did I know God had other plans. 10 years worth of plans to be exact. It has been one unbelievable journey, but I can truly say that the principles I wrote about in this book have held true. I've even found that many of the topics I covered in the book have spilled over into my married life.

I have been married for 5 years now. Like my sister had mentioned in our conversation in chapter 4, it has sometimes been hard work to maintain a healthy marriage. At the same time it is 100% worth it. Even through the roughest moments my wife and I have encountered I've never found myself wanting to go back to being single. That probably sounds ridiculous considering some of the most common advice I remember getting from married guys when I was single was, "(Insert any loud, obnoxious man's voice here) Ha! Don't get married!" Maybe you've heard that exact phrase before, or something similar. Perhaps someone has given you the advice, "Stay single as long as you can!" Many of the words of guidance we hear in our culture tend to convey the fact that marriage sucks the fun right out of our exhilarating, carefree single lives. I don't know about you, but much of my single time was fairly lonely and could definitely get miserable at times. I would go so far as to say that I have had more fun in my 5 years of marriage than in any other 5 year stretch of my life. Hey, God created the marriage institution, and from what I know about his creations they tend to end up being GOOD. To get a better picture about God's handiwork, read the first couple chapters of Genesis and notice what He says about the things He makes.

One thing I can't be grateful enough for is the fact that I'm not lonely anymore. Thank you, Jesus! The Psalmist was dead on when he said in Psalm 128, "Blessed are all those who fear the Lord, who walk in his ways. You will eat the fruit of your labor."

In case you are wondering, a few other things have changed for me since the writing of this awesome book. I have been teaching math at a local high school for 7 years now. Due to my wife encouraging me to get my masters in math, I recently started teaching at a local college, as well. And, throughout all of this, I have worked very hard to be the man God has called me to be, as I know many of you have too. I can't wait to see godly young men transform what people think about relationships into something great!

Fortunately, God has called us to be men of integrity. We are to treat women with the utmost dignity and respect. And just like anything that requires our respect, that sometimes means waiting for it. I hope this book has helped you as much as it helped me by giving you key areas to work on until that momentous day when you meet the love of your life!

Oh, and by the way, we have a little one on the way! By a miracle of God, our baby will be born at about the same time this book releases.

P.S. I still stink at pick-up lines. The one I used on my wife was, "Hey, do you know how much a male grizzly bear weighs?" Seriously! Thank you, babe for loving me anyway.

INTERVIEW QUESTIONS FOR DISCUSSION

The following selection of questions is intended to spark conversation. They are not meant to unearth the correct answer every time. I think it would be best to have a mediator (e.g. young adult pastor) ask the questions and a medium to large size group of young women and men. The questions should be light hearted and fun. Just remember that you don't have to argue your point. Throw your thoughts out there, but put more effort into interpreting how the opposite sex feels about given topics. You might learn something you never knew about how the other gender processes relationships. The following is a good example prayer to start everything off:

Jesus, thank you for allowing us to come together as we attempt to understand each other better. We know before we start that you have created men and women to be unique. May we value each other's opinions by not arguing, but by being honest and holding onto our integrity. We want to be open to not only hearing other's thoughts, but to really consider their worth. Let your Holy Spirit guide our conversation today so You are honored and pleased with us. Allow us to learn exactly what will help us become the women and men You intend for us to be. In Jesus' name, Amen!

Everybody Talk

Group questions for a co-ed group.

First Interview

1. How would you want your girlfriend/boyfriend to dress?
2. What do you think the opposite sex often gets wrong in the fashion department?
3. What is a good way to let the opposite sex know you are a Christian?
4. How much does it mean to you that a guy/girl smells good?
5. What kind of smell is the most important to you? (Clothing, Perfume/Cologne, Breath)
6. Give the opposite sex some hints by telling them what some of your favorite scents are.
7. What kind of compliments have the best effect on you?
8. Are there some kinds of compliments that you find unappealing?
9. How can you make sure your compliments are genuine?
10. If someone pays you a compliment, but you are not interested in the person how do you handle it?
11. What do you consider godly flirtation? How can the opposite sex let you know they like you?
12. How much does it matter to you that a guy/girl is confident in who they are?

13. Can confidence ever be unattractive?

14. Can attitude ever overshadow looks for you? Be honest.

15. What is the most appealing character trait to you? (Humor, honesty, intelligence.)

16. What would be an ideal first date for you?

17. Should the guy pay for a first date?

18. After marriage, is it necessary for one spouse to stay at home with the children while the other works?

19. What is one glaring thing you wish the opposite sex would do better?

Second Interview

1. What does being romantic mean to you?

2. Can being romantic go too far? If so, when do you feel like it has crossed the line?

3. What is your 'Love Language'? What can someone do that makes you feel appreciated?

4. How do you feel about friendship before a relationship?

5. How do you know whether to give up on a certain girl/guy, or keep pursuing a relationship with them?

6. Have you had many close opposite-sex friendships where you weren't interested in anything more?

7. How important is old-school chivalry to you? (e.g. opening doors for someone/having them opened for you)

8. What would you consider a completely romantic date? Does it involve being surprised? Would it be outdoors?

9. How can a person be creative and romantic?

10. Is it possible to be smothered by too much romance? Give an example.

11. What would you consider a great present from someone you aren't yet dating, or is that rushing it? How about from someone you've been dating for about a month?

12. Here's a big one: When do you feel is appropriate for a first kiss?

13. What types of kissing are appropriate before marriage, if any?

Third Interview

1. What is your view about marriage?

2. What do you think is a good age to get married? Why?

3. Is it always easy to talk to the opposite sex? If you say no, explain why it is sometimes difficult.

4. If you said yes to the last question, do you have any advice for people who find it to be more of a struggle?

5. What is a good way of building up your courage at being social?

6. Do you think excitement for each other typically dies down after marriage? Do many of the married couples you know still seem desperately in love? If you think of a couple that does seem that way, what do you think their secret is?

7. Is it possible to work on yourself now to be prepared to keep the fire going even after marriage? How?

8. What are some things you might miss about being single when you get married? Can you enjoy those things more right now if you focus on them?

9. What things can you get used to doing now that will probably score you some points in the married world?

10. How important do you think communication is in marriage? How can we work on that skill while we are single?

11. How essential is it that you and your boyfriend/girlfriend have the same beliefs about God?

12. Do you think marriage thrusts people closer to God than they were before, or do people usually stay the same?

13. Is it a good idea to get your relationship with God right before marriage? Why, or why not?

Fourth Interview

1. Do you think dating can be dangerous? If so, how?

2. Is dating scary to you? Why, or why not?

3. How many dates have you been on?

4. What makes it a date for you? Does the other person have to specify that you are going out on a date, or can it just be hanging out with someone?

5. Is there a great way to ask someone on a date? Have you ever heard any really horrible pick-up lines? Share some of them.

6. Talk about some great dates that you've had (if any) and what made them special.

7. Have you ever had a disastrous date? What went wrong?

8. Should guys pay for dates? If so, how many of the dates should the guy pick up the tab for?

9. How should a girl let the guy know if she wants to pay, or pitch in on the cost of a date?

10. What do you think about the following statement: 'A great date involves doing something memorable, not necessarily monetary.'?

11. How much personal space should be given on a first date?

12. How much does it matter if the person who picks you up has a clean car?

13. How can you be sure to make the person you are out on a date with the focus of the evening? How can a date be spoiled if your date is not the focus?

14. How is God involved in dating?

I hope everyone had fun tossing out ideas and communicating deeper truths. Remember to ponder the things that the opposite sex said, even if they seem odd to you, as God might just bring you someone with similar views!

Daniel Vasi lives with his beautiful wife and son, DJ, outside of Cleveland, Ohio. He holds a Master's degree in Mathematics from Cleveland State University and he teaches at Lorain County Community College. Daniel loves video games, traveling, and speaking about relationships. Daniel has started multiple Bible studies for young people through which he has been able to encourage and disciple many individuals. He currently helps lead Momentum, a college-age group of people passionate about discovering biblical truths.

For more visit:
www.christianbabealert.com
www.DanielVasi.com
Or on Facebook at Christian Babe Alert

VISIT THE LOCONEAL BLOG AT

www.loconeal.com

Breaking News
Forthcoming Releases
Links to Author Sites
Loconeal Events

www.ingramcontent.com/pod-product-compliance
Lightning Source LLC
Chambersburg PA
CBHW061652040426
42446CB00010B/1697